Texts *for* English Language Development

BENCHMARK EDUCATION COMPANY

Table of Contents

Why do laws continue to evolve?

James Madison, the
Father of the Constitution

My Language Objectives

- Understand the language of chronology
- Understand pronoun-antecedent agreement
- Use the past and past perfect verb tenses
- Write a first person reflection
- Combine sentences to connect ideas
- Use regular and irregular verbs

My Content Objectives

- Build my vocabulary related to governments and laws
- Understand why laws continue to evolve

a protest for civil rights

a Civil War battle

3

Creating the Constitution

by Benjamin Godfrey

In 1787, James Madison and fifty-six other delegates, or representatives, came to Philadelphia.... Their goal was to discuss changes to the government formed after the Revolutionary War.

James Madison

Madison had previously created the state constitution for Virginia. The delegates were interested in his ideas. Madison became the principal writer, or framer, of the Constitution.

Madison argued for a strong central government. At the time, the thirteen states had a lot of power... This made it hard for a national government to collect taxes or create a military.

After months of discussions, debates, and compromises, the delegates decided on a final document. They mostly followed Madison's Virginia Plan and established a stronger federal government.

1. ThinkSpeakListen

Explain why James Madison thought it was important to create a stronger central government.

Understand the Language of Chronology

In 1787, James Madison and fifty-six other delegates, or representatives, came to Philadelphia.

Madison had **previously** created the state constitution for Virginia.

At the time, the thirteen states had a lot of power.

After months of discussions, debates, and compromises, the delegates decided on a final document.

1 Madison creates state constitution for Virginia.

2 1787: Delegates meet in Philadelphia; thirteen states have a lot of power.

3 Delegates decide on a final document.

Soon after, Madison helped create the Bill of Rights. These are the first ten amendments, or additions, to the Constitution. The Bill of Rights lists many key freedoms Americans enjoy today, such as freedom of the press and free speech. For all his work on the Constitution, James Madison has been called the Father of the Constitution.

James Madison (1751–1836) became the fourth U.S. president in 1808. He served for two terms.

2. ThinkSpeakListen

What did James Madison do to earn the title "Father of the Constitution"?

President Lyndon Johnson's
Voting Rights Act Address

President Lyndon Johnson

At the height of the civil rights movement in the mid-1960s, President Lyndon Johnson gave a voting rights speech to Congress… Here are some excerpts from the speech.

"I speak tonight for the dignity of man and the destiny of democracy.

I urge every member of both parties—Americans of all religions and of all colors—from every section of this country—to join me in that cause…."

"Many of the issues of civil rights are very complex and most difficult. But about this there can and should be no argument. Every American citizen must have an equal right to vote."

"There is no reason which can excuse the denial of that right. There is no duty which weighs more heavily on us than the duty we have to ensure that right."

"Yet the harsh fact is that in many places in this country, men and women are kept from voting simply because they are Negroes...."

"No law that we now have on the books—and I have helped to put three of them there—can ensure the right to vote when local officials are determined to deny it."

"In such a case our duty must be clear to all of us. The Constitution says that no person shall be kept from voting because of his race or his color."

"We have all sworn an oath before God to support and to defend that Constitution.

We must now act in obedience to that oath."

3. ThinkSpeakListen

Why do you think it is important for all citizens to have the right to vote? Give reasons to support your opinion.

Susan B. Anthony

Few have influenced the United States Constitution as much as Susan B. Anthony (1820–1906). Throughout her life, she spoke out on topics ranging from forced labor to education to workers' rights. Several amendments to the Constitution benefited from her support, including the abolition of slavery....

Susan B. Anthony

Anthony banded together with others who shared her views. These included Elizabeth Cady Stanton and Lucretia Mott. In 1866 they established the American Equal Rights Association. Some members lobbied for a national amendment on women's suffrage....

In 1920, the Nineteenth Amendment to the Constitution granted women the right to vote in national elections. Though she wasn't alive to witness its passage, Susan B. Anthony's name became synonymous with the new amendment.

4. ThinkSpeakListen

Compare and contrast how Susan B. Anthony and President Lyndon Johnson fought for people's right to vote.

Understand Pronoun-Antecedent Agreement

	Singular Antecedent	Singular Pronoun
	James Madison (1751–1836) became the fourth U.S. president in 1808.	He served two terms.

	Plural Antecedent	Plural Pronoun
	After months of discussions, debates, and compromises, the delegates decided on a final document.	They mostly followed Madison's Virginia Plan and established a stronger federal government.

	Singular Antecedent	Singular Pronoun
	Few have influenced the United States Constitution as much as Susan B. Anthony (1820–1906).	Throughout her life, she spoke out on topics ranging from forced labor to education to workers' rights.

	Plural Antecedent	Plural Pronoun
	Anthony banded together with others who shared her views. These included Elizabeth Cady Stanton and Lucretia Mott.	In 1866 they established the American Equal Rights Association.

5. ThinkSpeakListen

Explain how James Madison, Lyndon Johnson, and Susan B. Anthony worked to protect people's rights. Make sure to use correct pronoun-antecedent agreement in your explanation.

The Dred Scott Decision by Monica Halpern

On March 6, 1857, the United States Supreme Court made a decision that stunned the nation. Dred Scott, an enslaved African American, had gone to court asking for his freedom in 1846.

Eleven years later, the court decided against him. The justices said that no black person, free or slave, could ever become a citizen of the United States. African Americans had no legal rights. Therefore, no black person could ask the court for his or her freedom. Scott had to remain enslaved....

Dred Scott

Who was the man at the center of this case? Dred Scott had been enslaved his whole life. He could not read or write....

Harriet and Dred Scott

As slaves, Scott and his family had no choice about where they lived. They were moved from place to place, sometimes to slave states or territories and sometimes to free places....

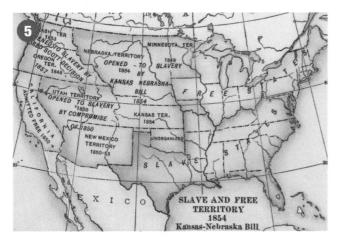

In April 1846,... Scott and his family were living in Missouri, a slave state. Scott asked a Missouri court for freedom for himself and his family. He claimed that they should be free because they had lived in a free state, Illinois...

The first trial began in June 1847 in Missouri State Court. Scott lost. In a new trial, the court found for Scott and his family, declaring them free... In 1852, [the Supreme Court of Missouri] overturned the earlier ruling...

Scott didn't give up. He continued his fight in the United States Circuit Court. However, in 1854 that court also ruled that Scott and his family were still slaves....

Still, Scott fought on. In December of 1854 he took his case to the highest court in the land, the United States Supreme Court.... By this time, people all over the nation were following the case....

6. ThinkSpeakListen

Explain why Dred Scott thought that he and his family should be freed from slavery.

Chief Justice Roger Taney

On March 6, 1857, the nine justices of the Supreme Court filed into the courtroom and took their seats. Chief Justice Roger Taney…said that because of Scott's race, he was not a citizen and had no right to sue under the Constitution.…

Henry Taylor Blow

What happened to the Scotts after they lost their case? The Blow family, descendants of Dred Scott's original owner, Peter Blow, purchased the Scotts and then set them free.…

Sadly, Scott did not have very long to enjoy his freedom. He became ill and died on September 17, 1858, about a year after gaining his freedom.

President Abraham Lincoln

Yet the Dred Scott case had considerable ramifications, or consequences. Abraham Lincoln used the case to help him win the presidential election in 1860.… In 1862, Lincoln issued the Emancipation Proclamation, which freed the slaves and ended slavery in the United States.

7. ThinkSpeakListen

How did the Dred Scott decision lead to the end of slavery in the United States?

Use the Past and Past Perfect Verb Tenses

The Dred Scott Decision

On March 6, 1857, the United States Supreme Court **made** a decision that stunned the nation. Dred Scott, an enslaved African American, **had gone** to court asking for his freedom in 1846.

1846: Dred Scott goes to court asking for his freedom.

1857: The Supreme Court makes a decision that stuns the nation.

Scott **asked** a Missouri court for freedom for himself and his family. He claimed that they should be free because they **had lived** in a free state.

Harriet and Dred Scott

Dred Scott and his family live in a free state.

Scott asks a Missouri court for freedom for himself and his family.

8. ThinkSpeakListen

Explain how the past and past perfect tenses can be used to explain the order in which events occur.

Mrs. Stowe and the President

Late in the year 1862, the writer Harriet Beecher Stowe traveled to Washington, D.C. for Thanksgiving dinner. Thousands of previously enslaved people attended the huge feast. They were primarily thankful for their freedom, but also for the chance to shake hands with the world-famous author of *Uncle Tom's Cabin*.

Harriet Beecher Stowe

The best-selling novel contained details of their lives that Mrs. Stowe had gathered from newspaper articles and firsthand accounts. For thousands of readers, each terrifying chapter was a call to action, a reason to fight for change....

The president knew the book had sparked great outrage around the country... That explained why he had invited Mrs. Stowe to meet with him.

"Why, Mrs. Stowe!" Lincoln exclaimed... "So you're the little woman who wrote the book that made this great war!"

Mrs. Stowe blushed. "I only hoped to speak the truth," she replied....

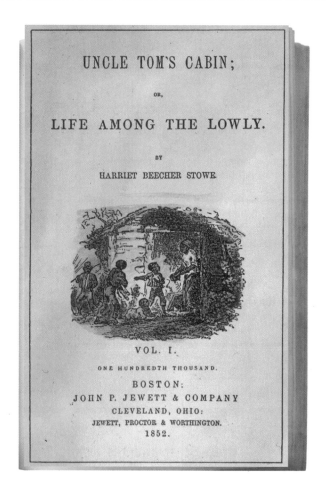

9. ThinkSpeakListen

Uncle Tom's Cabin was published before the Dred Scott case. How do you think Mrs. Stowe's writing might have influenced the case?

Writing to Sources

Writing Prompt

Now that you've read "The Dred Scott Decision," write a first person reflection from Dred Scott's point of view. Recount your thoughts and feelings about what has happened to you.

Source
Type of Writing
Focus of Writing

Sample First Person Reflection

I am tired. Harriet is tired. We keep asking ourselves: Should we quit our fight for freedom?

Strong opening introduces first person narrator and situation.

I often think of how we won back in 1847! It was glorious! But then the Supreme Court of Missouri overturned our victory, and our hearts sank. We asked: Can we try again?

Careful verb use helps the reader go between past and present.

I never gave up, though. In 1854, we lost in the United States Circuit Court.

Then we asked ourselves again: Can we take the claim to the Supreme Court?

A sequence of events unfolds naturally. Use transition words to show a sequence of events.

We did, but I'll never forget how I felt today when Justice Taney said that I had no right to sue. I thought, "Am I not a person, too?"

Narrator shares thoughts and feelings about events, using quotations.

I may be defeated, but I know the fight will go on.

Reflection has a sense of closure.

Thurgood Marshall's
Liberty Medal Acceptance Speech

Thurgood Marshall

Thurgood Marshall (1908–1993) was… the first African American to serve as a justice on the United States Supreme Court (1967–1991). He gave the following speech at Independence Hall in Philadelphia on July 4, 1992…

"What I'd like to do is to share a few stories, a few anecdotes, of people who have understood the meaning of liberty and struggled against the odds to become free."

"I think of these people because of the risks they have taken and the courage they have displayed. I value them not only because of the kind of people they were, but because of the kind of nation they insisted that we become…."

Heman Sweatt

"Do you remember Heman Sweatt? He was an ordinary man who had an extraordinary dream…"

"…to live in a world in which Afro-Americans and whites alike were afforded equal opportunity to sharpen their minds and to hone their skills."

"Unfortunately, officials at the University of Texas Law School did not share his vision…. They denied Heman Sweatt admission to law school solely because his color was not theirs."

"It was a devastating blow and a stinging rejection, a painful reminder of the chasm that separates white from Negro."

"But Heman Sweatt held on to what racism tried to snuff out: a sense of self and a recognition of place; a determination to attain the best and a refusal to settle for anything less."

10. ThinkSpeakListen

Compare and contrast the cases of Heman Sweatt and Dred Scott. How were they similar? How were they different?

"Heman Sweatt knew what whites and segregationists tried to forget, that none of us Afro, white, or blue, will ever rest until we are truly free…."

"Racism separates, but it never liberates. Hatred generates fear; and fear, once given a foothold, binds, consumes and imprisons. Nothing is gained from prejudice. No one benefits from racism…."

"Afro and white, rich and poor, educated and illiterate, our fates are bound together. We can run from each other but we cannot escape each other."

"We will only attain freedom if we learn to appreciate what is different, and muster the courage to discover what is fundamentally the same…."

11. ThinkSpeakListen

Compare and contrast the speeches given by Thurgood Marshal and Lyndon Johnson. Why did Marshall and Johnson think it was important to protect people's rights?

Combine Sentences to Connect Ideas

1. What I want to do is share a few stories, a few anecdotes, of people who have understood the meaning of liberty.

2. What I want to do is share a few stories, a few anecdotes, of people who have struggled against the odds to become free.

What I want to do is share a few stories, a few anecdotes, of people who have understood the meaning of liberty **and** struggled against the odds to become free.

1. Heman Sweatt **knew** what whites and segregationists tried to forget.

2. Heman Sweatt **knew** that none of us Afro, white, or blue, will ever rest until we are truly free.

Heman Sweatt **knew** what whites and segregationists tried to forget, that none of us Afro, white, or blue, will ever rest until we are truly free.

1. Racism separates.

2. It never liberates.

Racism separates, **but** it never liberates.

12. ThinkSpeakListen
Explain why a writer might choose to combine clauses.

The Presidential Medal of Freedom

In 1963, President John F. Kennedy established the Presidential Medal of Freedom. He wanted to pay tribute to men and women who promoted peace and upheld the Constitution. Individuals would be honored for their contributions to the arts as well....

President John F. Kennedy

Since then, more than five hundred people have received the medal. Civil rights leaders Thurgood Marshall and Dr. Martin Luther King Jr. were honored. So was Cesar Chavez for his struggle to obtain rights for farmworkers....

Marshall   King   Chavez

Today, the Medal of Freedom remains the nation's highest civilian honor. It reminds us that people of many talents and cultures work together to promote peace, justice, and liberty for all. Maybe one day you, too, will earn a Medal of Freedom for your accomplishments!

13. ThinkSpeakListen

Think of someone that you feel deserves the Presidential Medal of Freedom. Explain why you think this person deserves this honor.

Use Regular and Irregular Verbs

Present	No one **benefits** from racism….	Thurgood Marshall's Liberty Medal Acceptance Speech
Past	Several amendments to the Constitution **benefited** from her support, including the abolition of slavery….	Susan B. Anthony

Present	I **speak** tonight for the dignity of man and the destiny of democracy.	Voting Rights Act Address
Past	Throughout her life, she **spoke** out on topics ranging from forced labor to education to workers' rights.	Susan B. Anthony

Present	Every American citizen must **have** an equal right to vote.	Voting Rights Act Address
Past	He was an ordinary man who **had** an extraordinary dream…	Thurgood Marshall's Liberty Medal Acceptance Speech

14. ThinkSpeakListen
Explain the difference between regular and irregular verbs, and how to identify them in your reading.

Essential Question
Why do we value certain qualities in people?

Why do we value fairness?

My Language Objectives

- Understand verb tenses and contractions
- Understand and use interjections
- Use adverbials to describe manner
- Use prepositional phrases to describe place/direction
- Write an opinion essay

My Content Objectives

- Build vocabulary related to personal qualities
- Understand why we value certain qualities in people

Why do we value loyalty?

Why do we value kindness?

23

Becky Returns

an excerpt from *The Adventures of Tom Sawyer* by Mark Twain

The Adventures of Tom Sawyer is a classic American novel about a boy growing up on the Mississippi River in the late 1800s.… The protagonist of the novel, Tom Sawyer, is a mischievous character who frequently gets into trouble.…

Tom also has a love interest, Becky Thatcher… In the following excerpt from chapter 29, Becky has returned to town after vacation, and Tom wants to persuade her to spend time alone with him after a picnic at the ferry landing.…

Morning came, eventually, and by ten or eleven o'clock a giddy and rollicking company were gathered at Judge Thatcher's, and everything was ready for a start.… The last thing Mrs. Thatcher said to Becky was:

 "You'll not get back till late. Perhaps you'd better stay all night with some of the girls that live near the ferry-landing, child."

 "Then I'll stay with Susy Harper, mamma."

 "Very well. And mind and behave yourself and don't be any trouble."

Presently, as they tripped along, Tom said to Becky:

 "Say, I'll tell you what we'll do. 'Stead of going to Joe Harper's we'll climb right up the hill and stop at the Widow Douglas'. She'll have ice-cream! She has it most every day— dead loads of it. And she'll be awful glad to have us."…

 "But what will mamma say?"…

 "How'll she ever know?"…

 "I reckon it's wrong—but—"

1. ThinkSpeakListen

Based on this text, how would you describe the characters of Tom and Becky?

Understand Verb Tenses and Contractions

Contraction	Example from Text
I + will = **I'll**	Then **I'll** stay with Susy Harper, mamma.
You + will = **you'll**	**You'll** not get back till late.
She + will = **she'll**	**She'll** have ice-cream!
We + will = **we'll**	'Stead of going to Joe Harper's **we'll** climb right up the hill and stop at the Widow Douglas'.
It + is = **it's**	I reckon **it's** wrong—but—

 "But shucks! Your mother won't know, and so what's the harm? All she wants is that you'll be safe; and I bet you she'd 'a' said go there if she'd 'a' thought of it. I know she would!"

The Widow Douglas' splendid hospitality was a tempting bait. It and Tom's persuasions presently carried the day.

2. ThinkSpeakListen

Describe what you think might happen when Tom and Becky reach the Widow Douglas' house. Use contractions in your descriptions.

Games in the Woods

an excerpt from *The Adventures of Tom Sawyer* by Mark Twain

In this excerpt from chapter 8, Tom meets his friend Joe in the forest. The two boys each have a pretend sword and are dressed for adventurous play....

 "Hold! Who comes here into Sherwood Forest without my pass?"

 "Guy of Guisborne wants no man's pass.... Who art thou that dares to hold such language?"

 "I, indeed! I am Robin Hood,[1] as thy caitiff carcase[2] soon shall know."

 "Then art thou indeed that famous outlaw? Right gladly will I dispute with thee the passes of the merry wood. Have at thee!"

They took their lath swords, dumped their other traps on the ground, struck a fencing attitude, foot to foot, and began a grave, careful combat...

1 Robin Hood—an outlaw and hero of English folklore
2 caitiff carcase—a despicable person

 "Fall! fall! Why don't you fall?"

 "I sha'n't! Why don't you fall yourself? You're getting the worst of it."

 "Why, that ain't anything. I can't fall; that ain't the way it is in the book. The book says... You're to turn around and let me hit you in the back."

 "Now...you got to let me kill you. That's fair."

 "Why, I can't do that, it ain't in the book."

 "Well, it's blamed mean, that's all."

 "Well, say, Joe, you can be Friar Tuck or Much the miller's son, and lam me with a quarter-staff; or I'll be the Sheriff of Nottingham and you be Robin Hood a little while and kill me...."

The boys dressed themselves, hid their accoutrements, and went off grieving that there were no outlaws any more, and wondering what modern civilization could claim to have done to compensate for their loss.

3. ThinkSpeakListen

What valuable qualities does Tom Sawyer demonstrate in this story?

City Kid, Country Kid

Kinsey,

I just wanted to send a quick e-mail to see what's been happening this summer!... The highlight of my summer was volunteering with the Central Park Youth Crew. Four days a week, I worked with the conservation program doing landscape and maintenance chores.... I pulled tons of weeds! I've sort of been thinking that a career as an environmental scientist would be pretty amazing.

Well, that's it for me! Catch me up when you can spare a minute!

Jen

Jen,

My vacation highlight would probably be the horseback riding camp I attended in July. Since this was my second year, I focused more on training and on riding competition skills because I hope to participate in the 4-H Fair in October. It would be great if you could come down for that!

Later,
Kinsey

4. ThinkSpeakListen

Based on these e-mails, what do you think Jen and Kinsey's main qualities are?

Understand and Use Interjections

"**Say**, I'll tell you what we'll do."	
"But **shucks!** Your mother won't know, and so what's the harm?"	
"**Hold!** Who comes here into Sherwood Forest without my pass?"	
"I, **indeed!** I am Robin Hood, as thy caitiff carcase soon shall know."	
"**Why,** I can't do that, it ain't in the book."	
"**Well,** it's blamed mean, that's all."	

5. ThinkSpeakListen

Think of a time when you have used interjections. What was the situation? What kind of feelings were you trying to communicate?

Camp-Life

an excerpt from *The Adventures of Tom Sawyer* by Mark Twain

In the following excerpt from chapter 14, Tom, Joe, and Huck have taken a raft and run away to Jackson's Island, a small island on the Mississippi River, where they enjoy a life of freedom and adventure for several days. One day, they hear a cannon go off in the distance....

"What is it!" exclaimed Joe, under his breath.

"I wonder," said Tom in a whisper.

"'Tain't thunder," said Huckleberry, in an awed tone, "becuz thunder—"

"Hark!" said Tom. "Listen—don't talk."

They waited a time that seemed an age, and then the same muffled boom troubled the solemn hush.

"Let's go and see."

They sprang to their feet and hurried to the shore toward the town.… The little steam ferry-boat was about a mile below the village, drifting with the current.…

Presently a great jet of white smoke burst from the ferryboat's side, and as it expanded and rose in a lazy cloud, that same dull throb of sound was borne to the listeners again.

"I know now!" exclaimed Tom; "somebody's drownded!"

"That's it!" said Huck; "they done that last summer, when Bill Turner got drownded; they shoot a cannon over the water…"

"By jings, I wish I was over there, now," said Joe.

"I do too," said Huck. "I'd give heaps to know who it is."

6. ThinkSpeakListen

Based on the text and illustrations, how would you describe the characters of Tom, Joe, and Huck?

The boys still listened and watched. Presently a revealing thought flashed through Tom's mind, and he exclaimed:

"Boys, I know who's drownded—it's us!"

They felt like heroes in an instant. Here was a gorgeous triumph; they were missed; they were mourned; hearts were breaking on their account; tears were being shed…

The pirates returned to camp. They were jubilant with vanity over their new grandeur and the illustrious trouble they were making.…

But when the shadows of night closed them in, they gradually ceased to talk, and sat gazing into the fire, with their minds evidently wandering elsewhere.

7. ThinkSpeakListen

Why did the boys feel "like heroes" at the end of this story?

Use Adverbials to Describe Manner

"What is it!" exclaimed Joe, **under his breath.**	
"I wonder," said Tom **in a whisper**.	
"'Tain't thunder," said Huckleberry, **in an awed tone**, "becuz thunder—"	
But when the shadows of night closed them in, they **gradually** ceased to talk, and sat gazing into the fire, with their minds evidently wandering elsewhere.	

8. ThinkSpeakListen

Use adverbials to describe how you would talk in a library, in your classroom, and at a large concert or sporting event.

All Together Now!

Camp Sky Rock buzzed with campers' voices as they discussed their ideas for a mural. It seemed as if everyone was talking at once—everyone, that is, except Caleb, who sat quietly against the wall sketching in his notebook....

No sooner was an idea called out than Caleb added it to his ever-growing sketch. Kai glanced down at the notebook and shouted, "Wow, Caleb, that's awesome! Hey, guys, look at this! This should be our mural!"...

Caleb made the sketch on large, mural-sized paper, and each boy signed up for the part of the mural he wanted to paint. Unnoticed, their counselor, Stan, used his cell phone to take a photo of them at work. When the painting was finished, Stan handed them a printout of the photo. "Talk about cooperation—these are great examples!" he said, pointing to the mural and the kids in the photo. "Outstanding!"

9. ThinkSpeakListen

Which character in this story is most like Tom Sawyer?

Use Prepositional Phrases to Describe Place/Direction

They sprang to their feet and hurried **to the shore toward the town**.	
The little steam ferry-boat was about a mile **below the village**, drifting with the current.	
Presently a great jet of white smoke burst **from the ferryboat's side**, and as it expanded and rose in a lazy cloud, that same dull throb of sound was borne **to the listeners** again.	
But when the shadows of night closed them in, they gradually ceased to talk, and sat gazing **into the fire**, with their minds evidently wandering elsewhere.	

10. ThinkSpeakListen

Use prepositional phrases to describe how you get to school in the morning.

Tom's Secret

an excerpt from *The Adventures of Tom Sawyer* by Mark Twain

In the following excerpts, Tom and Huck make a plan to search for a chest of gold coins that a thief (disguised as a Spaniard) and his accomplice have hidden somewhere in town. The boys spied the two men digging up the gold and overheard their plans to hide it….

 "Hello, Huck!"

 "Hello, yourself."

Silence, for a minute.

 "Tom, if we'd 'a' left the blame tools at the dead tree, we'd 'a' got the money. Oh, ain't it awful!"

 "'Tain't a dream, then, 'tain't a dream! Somehow I most wish it was. Dog'd if I don't, Huck."

 "What ain't a dream?"

 "Oh, that thing yesterday. I been half thinking it was."

 "Dream! If them stairs hadn't broke down you'd 'a' seen how much dream it was! I've had dreams enough all night—with him going for me all through 'em, rot him!"

 "No, not rot him. Find him! Track the money!"

 "Tom, we'll never find him.… I'd feel mighty shaky if I was to see him, anyway."

 "Well, so'd I; but I'd like to see him, anyway—and track him out—to his Number Two."

 "Number Two, yes, that's it. I been thinking 'bout that. But I can't make nothing out of it. What do you reckon it is?"…

 "Lemme think a minute. Here—it's the number of a room—in a tavern, you know!"

 "Oh, that's the trick! They ain't only two taverns. We can find out quick."…

11. ThinkSpeakListen
Why do you think Tom thought his encounter with the thief was a dream?

Tom was off at once.... He found that in the best tavern, No. 2 had long been occupied by a young lawyer... In the less ostentatious house, No 2 was a mystery. The tavern-keeper's young son said it was kept locked all the time...

 "That's what I've found out, Huck. I reckon that's the very No. 2 we're after."

 "I reckon it is, Tom. Now what you going to do?"

 "I'll tell you.... you get hold of all the doorkeys you can find, and I'll nip all of auntie's, and the first dark night we'll go there and try 'em. And mind you, keep a lookout... If you see him, you just follow him; and if he don't go to that No. 2, that ain't the place."...

 "It's so, Tom, it's so. I'll foller him; I will, by jingoes!"

 "Now you're talking! Don't you ever weaken, Huck, and I won't."

12. ThinkSpeakListen

How would you describe Tom's behavior in this excerpt? What does this behavior tell you about Tom's character?

Understand Verb Tenses and Contractions

Contraction	Example from Text
had + not = **hadn't**	If them stairs **hadn't** broke down you'd 'a' seen how much dream it was!
I + have = **I've**	**I've** had dreams enough all night…
I + would = **I'd**	**I'd** feel mighty shaky if I was to see him…
That + is = **that's**	**That's** what I've found out, Huck.
You + are = **you're**	Now **you're** talking!
Do + not = **don't** Will + not = **won't**	**Don't** you ever weaken, Huck, and I **won't**.

13. ThinkSpeakListen

Form and use contractions to describe something you did last week, and something you plan to do next week. Ask a partner about his or her plans.

Twain and Tom

Samuel Clemens was born on November 30, 1835. No one could have guessed that one day this child would become the beloved writer Mark Twain. His novel *The Adventures of Tom Sawyer* has been read by millions all over the world....

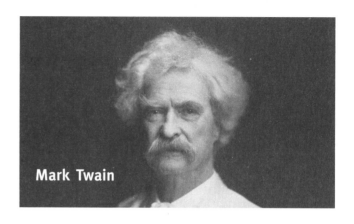

Mark Twain

It's no secret that Twain's hometown of Hannibal, Missouri, was the inspiration for St. Petersburg, the river town where Tom Sawyer lived. Hannibal is on the Mississippi River. Steamboats on the river were an everyday sight. In fact, the pen name Mark Twain means "twelve feet of water" in steamboat lingo....

It may be that Twain's love of adventure was what he drew on most when creating Tom Sawyer. Tom and his friends explored Jackson Island.... In real life, the young boy who would become Mark Twain explored Glasscock Island with his pals. In many ways, reading about Tom Sawyer gives readers a glimpse into the real life of Mark Twain.

14. ThinkSpeakListen

If "reading about Tom Sawyer gives readers a glimpse into the real life of Mark Twain," what else can you conclude about Mark Twain's childhood?

Writing to Sources

Question
Purpose of Writing
Focus of Writing

Writing Prompt

Based on what you have read in this unit, what do you think is Tom Sawyer's most admirable character trait? Write an opinion essay in which you answer this question. Support your opinion with details from one of the texts you have read in this unit.

Sample Opinion Essay

The character of Tom Sawyer displays many admirable (and not so admirable) qualities in *The Adventures of Tom Sawyer*. In my opinion, Tom's most admirable character trait is that he is fair to his friends. Even though he likes to be the leader, Tom gives his friends a chance to share in the fun.

In "Games in the Woods," Tom and Joe play Robin Hood. Tom pretends to be Robin, and Joe plays Robin's enemy, Guy of Guisborne. They play "by the book," meaning that their story has to go a certain way. Since Robin is supposed to beat Guy, Joe lets Tom defeat him in battle.

However, Joe wants to win, too. So, Tom offers to let Joe be Robin Hood and have a turn winning the battle. In this way, both boys get to have fun. Afterwards, they walk home "grieving that there were no outlaws any more." Tom shows he's a good friend by treating Joe fairly and letting him be Robin Hood.

So, even though Tom is often the leader, he always treats his friends fairly. In my opinion, this is his best trait, and it makes him a good friend.

Your introduction should introduce the topic, state your opinion, and give the reader a brief idea of what you will write about.

Your body paragraphs should provide reasons that support your opinion.

Your conclusion should restate your opinion, and provide a closing statement.

Essential Question

How do we decide which resources we should develop?

We consider what we need.

My Language Objectives

- Use the language of cause and effect
- Recognize prepositional phrases
- Connect two ideas in a sentence
- Research to write an informative essay
- Use the past and present verb tenses
- Use adverbs to describe verbs and adjectives

My Content Objectives

- Build vocabulary related to the development of resources
- Understand the choices we make in developing resources

We consider what we can use.

We consider the environment.

43

The Structure of a Corn Plant

by Mark Felkonian

First cultivated thousands of years ago by the early inhabitants of what is now Mexico, corn is an adaptable plant that can grow in different types of climates.

As people migrated, they grew corn in other regions. As a result, the crop soon spread across the continent....

Corn is a tall, green, leafy plant most often supported by a single stem, or stalk...

The ear usually grows out from a leaf node in the middle of the stalk....

When pollen grains from the tassel fall on the exposed silks of the corn ear, pollination occurs....

After fertilization, the rows of eggs grow into kernels.

1. ThinkSpeakListen

Describe what a cornfield looks like, and what an individual corn plant looks like.

44

Use the Language of Cause and Effect

<u>As</u> people migrated, they grew corn in other regions.	
<u>When</u> pollen grains from the tassel fall on the exposed silk of the corn ear, pollination occurs.	
<u>After</u> fertilization, the rows of eggs grow into kernels.	

2. ThinkSpeakListen

Answer the following question: What do you think were some of the long-term effects of the spread of corn across North America? Use the language of cause and effect in your answer.

The Past and Future of a Crop

by Amelia Millilo, Kelly Gold, and Brett Berger

Earth is a system in which energy from the sun constantly cycles living and nonliving matter through various processes.

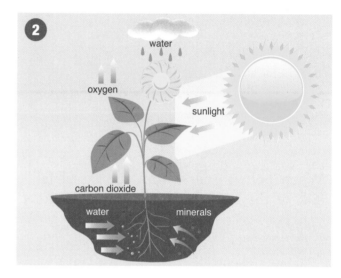

For example, plants, such as corn, are called producers. They use the sun's energy to make food through a chemical process known as photosynthesis.

Animals, such as humans, are called consumers. They eat plants...in order to obtain the energy they need to function.

Before the emergence of civilizations, early humans hunted and gathered food.... They simply gathered whatever was growing and ate it.

Through cultivation, humans… developed an understanding of how to breed certain seeds to yield more productive and desirable crops for consumption.

Corn is one such crop that has been cultivated over time to produce optimum traits for survival and use.

Today, corn is a major crop…used to feed humans and livestock.

Therefore, corn is grown directly to provide humans with food energy—and has been for thousands of years.

3. ThinkSpeakListen

Answer the following question: Why is corn such an important crop?

Paul Bunyan and the Great Popcorn Blizzard

Paul Bunyan traveled through the great Midwest with his sidekick, Babe the Blue Ox. At that time, the land was covered with forests as far as the eye could see…

One spring, Paul and his team cleared giant oak trees from the forests of Iowa so that farmers could plant corn. When summer came, the weather was so hot you could fry eggs on a rock…. The corn kernels grew so large they looked like balloons about to burst….

On a scorching day when the temperature was above 110 degrees, the corn started popping! All across Iowa, corn kernels popped out of their ears. Soon the entire state was covered with popcorn thirteen feet deep!

4. ThinkSpeakListen

Answer the following question: Why do people enjoy tall tales, such as this one, even though they are not true?

Recognize Prepositional Phrases

Text	Effects
"The Structure of a Corn Plant"	As people migrated, they grew corn <u>in other regions</u>.
	<u>As a result</u>, the crop soon spread <u>across the continent</u>.
"The Past and Future of a Crop"	<u>Through cultivation</u>, humans … developed an understanding <u>of how</u> to breed certain seeds to yield more productive and desirable crops <u>for consumption</u>.
	Corn is one such crop that has been cultivated <u>over time</u> to produce optimum traits <u>for survival and use</u>.

5. ThinkSpeakListen

Explain how a prepositional phrase is formed, and identify some prepositional phrases in "Paul Bunyan and the Great Popcorn Blizzard."

A Short History of a Special Plant
by Laura McDonald

The first Native American corn farmers used the seeds from the healthiest corn plants to grow their crops. This selective breeding improved their crop yield.

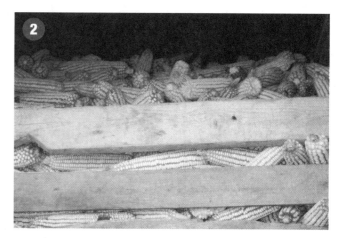

When farmers realized that they could plant a surplus of corn and not hurt their fields, they grew larger crops and stored the leftover corn…

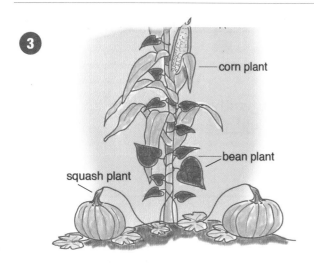

corn plant

bean plant

squash plant

Early farmers planted their fields with three plants—corn, squash, and beans—together. Each plant helped the other grow…

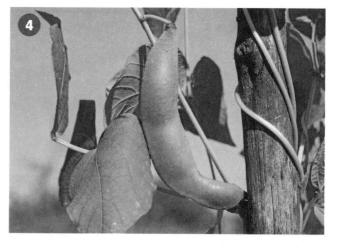

Corn was a strong and vertical plant… so the beans could curl up around its stalk. In turn, the beans fixed nitrogen in their roots, helping restore the soil.

Meanwhile, the squash leaves spread out on the ground and retained moisture in the soil for the other plants....

The end result was a healthy crop that yielded a variety of nutritious plants and also maintained the integrity of the soil....

With industrialization in the 1800s, new farming methods and technology began to change agriculture....

In the late 1800s scientists developed hybrid corn. Fertilizing one variety of corn with pollen from another variety makes hybrids....

6. ThinkSpeakListen

Summarize the methods used by the first Native American corn farmers to improve their crop yields.

This corn mixed favorable genetic traits and led to healthier varieties of corn and higher, faster yields….

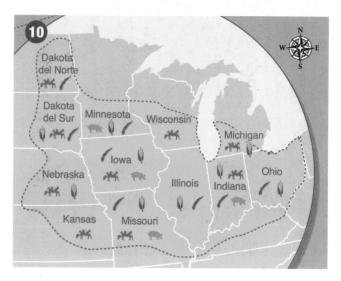

Today, corn is a staple crop of the Midwestern United States. Ninety-five percent of corn acreage is planted with hybrid corn…

Almost all corn in the United States grows from hybrid seeds. Hybrid corn may even contain genetic material, or DNA, from other species altogether.

Scientists have added DNA that makes corn more resistant to insects and drought.

7. ThinkSpeakListen

Answer the following question: In what ways are the methods used by today's farmers different from the methods of the first Native American corn farmers?

Connect Two Ideas in a Sentence

Idea #1	Idea #2	Sentences That Connect Ideas
Corn was a strong and vertical plant ...	so the beans could curl up around the stalk.	**Compound sentence with coordinating conjunction:** Corn was a strong and vertical plant, so the beans could curl up around the stalk.
When farmers realized that they could plant a surplus of corn and not hurt their fields,	they grew larger crops.	**Complex sentence with subordinating conjunction:** When farmers realized that they could plant a surplus of corn and not hurt their fields, they grew larger crops.
Scientists have added DNA	that makes corn more resistant to insects and drought.	**Complex sentence with relative pronoun:** Scientists have added DNA that makes corn more resistant to insects and drought.

8. ThinkSpeakListen

Answer the following questions: Why might an author want to combine two ideas into one sentence? Why might an author choose to keep ideas in separate sentences?

The Union of Corn and Bean

Long ago, when plants and animals had voices, a plant named Corn grew in a lovely garden. Corn was tall and handsome... Yet there were moments when his spirit was heavy...

One evening, as Corn was enjoying the sunset, he saw two butterflies happily whispering and laughing. Suddenly, he understood why he felt unhappy at times. He was lonely... Corn sang a song about his loneliness.

The following morning, a pretty Squash plant approached him. "I heard your song," she explained, "and I would happily live with you and marry you."

However, Corn realized that the two of them would not be a suitable match. "Although you are a splendid plant, we are not compatible," he replied. "You wander around the ground, while I remain in one spot, growing tall...."

Meanwhile, a Bean plant happened to overhear their conversation. She planted herself next to Corn...and soon they were happily married.

9. ThinkSpeakListen

Answer the following questions: Why might Squash be a bad match for Corn? Why might Bean be a good match for him?

Write to Sources

Building Research Skills

Imagine that you are conducting research to explain new ways to create ethanol. One of your guiding research questions is: Why do scientists think it is necessary to develop new ways to create ethanol? Read and take notes to gather facts and details from two or more approved digital sources to answer this question. List your sources.

Research Question

Sources You Will Use

Final Product

Guiding Research Question: Why do scientists think it is necessary to develop new ways to create ethanol?

Source: Renewable Fuels Association, "Ethanol Facts: Environment"

http://www.ethanolrfa.org/pages/ethanol-facts-environment

Author: Dr. Steffen Mueller

Date visited: November 13, 2014

Notes:

Ethanol is better for the environment than gasoline because

- it is biodegradable;
- it creates less greenhouse gas.

Source: U.S. Department of Energy: Alternative Fuels Data Center, "Ethanol Benefits and Considerations"

http://www.afdc.energy.gov/fuels/ethanol_benefits.html

Author: not listed

Date visited: November 13, 2014

Notes:

Benefits of ethanol:

- It is produced locally.
- Its production creates jobs.
- It emits less carbon dioxide than gasoline.

The Science of Growing Food

The Case for Keeping Corn Number 1   by Carla Corriols

Today, corn is the most widely grown crop in the United States. If Americans are smart, they'll keep it that way....

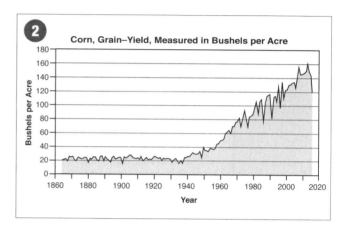

Corn is a productive crop. It has been bred and modified to produce astoundingly high yields compared with most other crops in the United States.

It is an extremely resilient crop as well. It can flourish in a variety of climates....

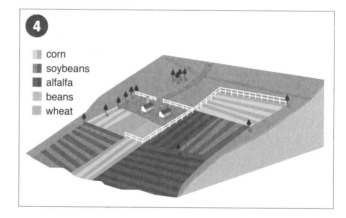

In the past, Americans grew different crops to meet the needs of different markets.... By consolidating crops and focusing efforts on corn, American growers have cut costs...

10. ThinkSpeakListen

Recount two reasons that Corriols wants us to keep corn the number one crop.

Some people are calling for a return to the more diversified farming practices of the past. They argue that soil is depleted by the two-crop corn-soybean rotation.

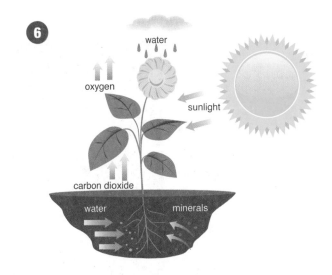

However…the high photosynthetic rate of corn plants means more organic matter is returned annually to the soil with corn than with other crops.

Did Farmers of the Past Know More Than We Do?

by Verlyn Klinkenborg

field of oat plants

A couple years ago, I saw a small field of oats growing in northwest Iowa—a 40-acre patch in a sea of genetically modified corn and soybeans.…

The purpose of that patch of oats was manure mitigation. The waste that had been sprayed on that field came from a hog confinement operation…

oats

alfalfa

rows of corn and soybean plants

Oats used to be a common sight all over the Midwest. They were often sown with alfalfa as a "nurse crop" to provide some cover for alfalfa seedlings…

Since then two things have happened. All the animals have moved indoors… And the number of crops has dwindled to exactly two: corn and soybeans.

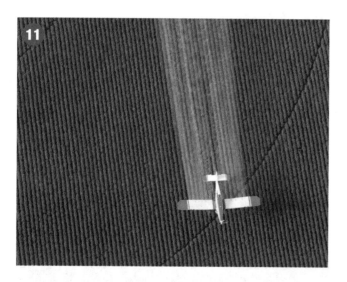

A modern rotation includes only corn, soybeans, fertilizer, and pesticides.…

And because those chemicals depend on fossil energy, the entire system is inherently unsustainable. What farmers used to return to the soil…they now must purchase.

11. ThinkSpeakListen

Summarize the opinions of Carla Corriols and Verlyn Klinkenborg.

Use the Past and Present Verb Tenses

Text	Simple Past	Simple Present
"The Past and Future of a Crop"	Before the emergence of civilizations, early humans <u>hunted</u> and <u>gathered</u> food.	Earth <u>is</u> a system in which energy from the sun constantly <u>cycles</u> living and nonliving matter through various processes.
"A Short History of a Special Plant"	In the late 1800s scientists <u>developed</u> hybrid corn. This corn <u>mixed</u> favorable genetic traits and <u>led</u> to healthier varieties of corn and higher, faster yields…	Fertilizing one variety of corn with pollen from another variety <u>makes</u> hybrids. Almost all corn in the United States <u>grows</u> from hybrid seeds.
"The Science of Growing Food"	A couple years ago, I <u>saw</u> a small field of oats growing in northwest Iowa—a 40-acre patch in a sea of genetically modified corn and soybeans. The purpose of that patch of oats <u>was</u> manure mitigation.	The entire system <u>is</u> inherently unsustainable.

12. ThinkSpeakListen

Summarize some things about corn that you have learned this week. Use simple present verbs and simple past verbs in your summary.

The World's Only Corn Palace

Many palaces around the world have been built for kings and queens. However, there's only one palace that was built to celebrate corn. Located in Mitchell, South Dakota, the middle of America, it's the one and only Corn Palace.

The Corn Palace looks like a Russian castle. Inside and out, it's decorated with large, colorful murals made of corn, grain, and grass. At first glance, the murals look like mosaics made of small tiles. On closer inspection, though, you see that they're made of different colored corn!

The murals on the outside of the building are changed yearly to reflect different themes. For example, past themes have been "Everyday Heroes" and "America's Destinations." The murals inside the palace are changed about every ten years.

13. ThinkSpeakListen

Answer the following question: Why might people want to make art out of corn?

Use Adverbs to Describe Verbs and Adjectives

Text	Sentence with an Adverb	Verb the Adverb Modifies
"The Past and Future of a Crop"	Earth is a system in which energy from the sun <u>constantly</u> cycles living and nonliving mater through various processes.	cycles
	They <u>simply</u> gathered whatever was growing and ate it.	gathered

Text	Sentence with an Adverb	Adjective the Adverb Modifies
"The Science of Growing Food"	It has been bred and modified to produce <u>astoundingly</u> high yields compared with most other crops in the United States.	high
	It is an <u>extremely</u> resilient crop as well.	resilient
	The entire system is <u>inherently</u> unsustainable.	unsustainable

14. ThinkSpeakListen

Find other adverbs in "The Science of Growing Food" and determine what words they modify.

Essential Question

How can other perspectives help us evaluate the world?

People have different perspectives on historical events.

My Language Objectives

- Use adverbials to describe time
- Understand the language of comparison
- Use conjunctions to connect ideas
- Form and use irregular verbs
- Understand verbs and verb phrases: modal auxiliaries
- Write an opinion essay

My Content Objectives

- Build vocabulary related to different perspectives
- Understand how other perspectives can help us evaluate the world

Readers have different perspectives on stories.

Characters have different perspectives on story events.

I Hear America Singing

by Walt Whitman

I hear America singing, the varied carols I hear,

Those of mechanics, each one singing his as it should be blithe and strong,

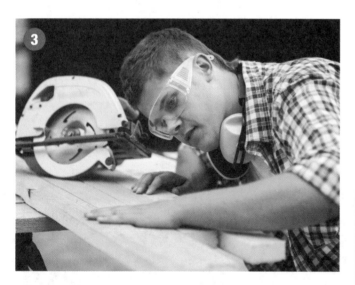

The carpenter singing his as he measures his plank or beam,

The mason singing his as he makes ready for work, or leaves off work.

1. ThinkSpeakListen

What do you think the narrator of the poem means when he says he hears people "singing"?

Use <u>Adverbials</u> to Describe Time

The carpenter singing his <u>as he measures his plank or beam,</u>

The mason singing his <u>as he makes ready for work, or leaves off work…</u>

I, Too
by Langston Hughes

I, too, sing America.

I am the darker brother.
They send me to eat in the kitchen
<u>When company comes,</u>
But I laugh,
And eat well,
And grow strong.

Langston Hughes

2. ThinkSpeakListen
How is Langston Hughes's view of America different from that of Walt Whitman?

Gold Country

an excerpt from *The Journal of Wong Ming-Chung: A Chinese Miner, California, 1852* by Laurence Yep

The Journal of Wong Ming-Chung…is told from the perspective of "Runt," a bookish young teen who travels alone to California from his native China to help his uncle search for gold during the California Gold Rush. These are excerpts from his journal entries written soon after he arrives.

The Golden Mountain is stranger, scarier, funnier, sadder and more wonderful than I ever imagined….

When we got off the ship, I thought I was in the middle of a forest. Except I could hear the ocean. Then I realized the tall poles were the masts of ships.

I was surrounded by hundreds of empty boats. They jam the harbor like fish in my village pond. I bet I could have walked from one deck to another across the bay.

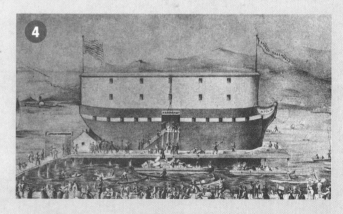

I didn't see any sailors. Instead, I saw laundry hanging from lines as if people were using the boats as houses. Then I saw one ship that literally had a house built on top of it….

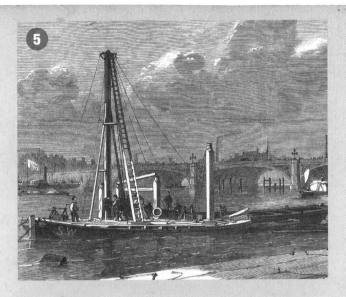

5

Big, loud machines were pounding logs vertically into the mud a half-kilometer from shore. Real houses perched on top of logs that had already been driven in.

6

Men and machines were filling in the shoreline to make more space. In some places, they weren't even bothering to move the ship, but were just filling the dirt around it....

7

First City nestles at the foot of steep hills between the shore and the hillsides. A few houses lie scattered on the slopes. Instead of building on the hills, they're expanding into the water.

8

Though it's summer, the air is as chilly here as winter back at home. I have to stop now. They're calling for us to register.

3. ThinkSpeakListen

Based on his description, how is "First City" different from Wong Ming-Chung's home in China?

Annie's New Homeland

"We're coming into New York Harbor!"

Fifteen-year-old Annie perked up at her brother's words. The voyage by steamship from Ireland to the United States had been long and difficult. It was a bitter, cold day in January 1892, but she and her two brothers rushed to the deck. They gaped at the welcoming Statue of Liberty....

The steamship docked, but before the passengers were allowed ashore, they had to pass through customs at Ellis Island. They waited in long lines in the crowded Registry Room to be examined by doctors... Another long line took them to a customs officer who looked over their documents.

Gathering their belongings, the three headed bravely into New York City. Annie would look for work as a cook or a maid, while her brothers would begin the dangerous work of building bridges and railroads. Life would not be easy, but Annie knew they'd survive and contribute to their new homeland.

4. ThinkSpeakListen

Summarize the steps Annie had to take before she was allowed to settle in New York City.

Understand the Language of Comparison

Example from Text

I am the <u>darker</u> brother.	 Langston Hughes
The Golden Mountain is <u>stranger</u>, <u>scarier</u>, <u>funnier</u>, <u>sadder</u> and <u>more</u> wonderful <u>than</u> I ever imagined.	
They jam the harbor <u>like</u> fish in my village pond.	
Though it's summer, the air is <u>as</u> chilly here <u>as</u> winter back at home.	

5. ThinkSpeakListen

Using the language of comparison, compare Wong Ming-Chung's and Annie's first experiences in America.

Justice in Eatonville

an excerpt from *Zora and Me*   by Victoria Bond and T. R. Simon

Zora and Me (2010) is a fictional account of the early life of Zora Neale Hurston (1891–1960), the African American author, anthropologist, and folklorist.... The novel, narrated by Zora's friend Carrie, follows the two fourth-grade girls and their friend Teddy as they attempt to solve a murder mystery. In this excerpt from Chapter 25 of the novel, Zora and Carrie confront Joe Clarke, the town sheriff and owner of the general store. The girls tell him what they suspect about the incident and the people involved: Gold, a beautiful woman who comes back to town on the arm of a white suitor; Ivory, a turpentine worker who arrives one day in search of Gold; and Mr. Pendir, an elderly man whom Zora believes to be "half-gator" and "half-man."

Now that we knew who Gold and Ivory were, and how Joe Clarke knew them, and maybe who had taken Ivory's life, there was one piece of the puzzle still missing.

And Zora, determined to know everything, demanded the final answer. "What about Mr. Pendir? Did he want to be a gator more than a man?"...

"Yes and no," Joe Clarke said...

② "His mama's family were poor sharecroppers, and they didn't need another mouth to feed, so he was raised working for white folks, but like a slave, not like a child."

"He grew up feeling like a whipping post.... He knew how to work wood, but he never learned how to be friendly with folks, and never learned how to let folks be friendly with him...."

③ Mr. Clarke stood and stretched his big bones. "This desk right here, Mr. Pendir made it for me."

"He was blessed with the power to take plain wood—scraps too small to be worth much to anyone—and carve them and shape them and paint them into something else."

6. ThinkSpeakListen

Why do you think Mr. Pendir "never learned how to be friendly with folks"?

4

He reached into a drawer and drew out a lion mask so detailed that Zora and I gasped. "Mr. Pendir breathed life into wood.

"When his fears threatened to swallow him up, he faced them down with the masks he made. His art scared off his fear."…

5

Zora and I sat with that a moment. Joe Clarke's lips spread across his face in a closed-mouth smile. It was a sad smile, but reassuring.

"I'm going to do justice, girls, but sometimes justice works better in silence…. Don't tell anyone else what you know. Let justice take its course now."

7. ThinkSpeakListen

What do you think Mr. Clarke meant when he said that Mr. Pendir's "art scared off his fear"?

Use Conjunctions to Connect Ideas

	Conjunctions	
"His mama's family were poor sharecroppers." "They didn't need another mouth to feed." "He was raised working for white folks." "He was raised like a slave, not like a child."	**and** **so** **but**	"His mama's family were poor sharecroppers, **and** they didn't need another mouth to feed, **so** he was raised working for white folks, **but** like a slave, not like a child."
"He knew how to work wood." "He never learned how to be friendly with folks." "He never learned how to let folks be friendly with him."	**but** **and**	"He knew how to work wood, **but** he never learned how to be friendly with folks, **and** never learned how to let folks be friendly with him."

8. ThinkSpeakListen

What is your opinion of "Justice in Eatonville"? Support your opinion with specific reasons, and use conjunctions to connect your ideas.

Zora Neale Hurston

The Zora in the novel *Zora and Me* is based on a real person—the author Zora Neale Hurston.... She was born in Alabama in 1891 but spent her childhood in Florida. Zora eventually left the South. She was bound for Harlem, an African American neighborhood in New York City.... Over the next thirty years, she published four novels, two books of folklore,... and a number of short stories and plays. She won many awards for her work.

Hurston was a rare kind of person who could walk into a room and command immediate attention. She was smart and amusing, and people liked her.

Zora Neale Hurston

She spent years collecting and publishing the folklore and stories of southern Americans. Without her work, many of these traditional stories might have been lost forever. Her own stories and novels, however, were based on her life growing up as an African American in the rural South.

Hurston eventually returned to her beloved Florida, where she died in 1960. Her gravestone reads, "Zora Neale Hurston: A Genius of the South."

9. ThinkSpeakListen

Compare this description of Zora Neale Hurston with the character of Zora in "Justice in Eatonville." How are they similar?

Form and Use Irregular Verbs

Example from "Justice in Eatonville"	Present Tense	Past Tense
Now that we **knew** who Gold and Ivory were, and how Joe Clarke knew them, and maybe who had taken Ivory's life, there was one piece of the puzzle still missing.	know	knew
"He **grew** up feeling like a whipping post."	grow	grew
"At first folks tried to bring him into the circle of town life, but he just couldn't **put** his hurt and mistrust away."	put	put
Mr. Clarke **stood** and stretched his big bones.	stand	stood
"This desk right here, Mr. Pendir **made** it for me."	make	made
He reached into a drawer and **drew** out a lion mask so detailed that Zora and I gasped.	draw	drew

Example from "Zora Neale Hurston"	Present Tense	Past Tense
Zora eventually **left** the South.	leave	left
She **won** many awards for her work.	win	won
She **spent** years collecting and publishing the folklore and stories of southern Americans.	spend	spent

10. ThinkSpeakListen
Use these irregular verbs to describe the life of Zora Neale Thurston.

Asparagus

an excerpt from *Esperanza Rising* by Pam Muñoz Ryan

Esperanza Rising (2000) tells the story of a thirteen-year-old girl who is living a life of privilege in Mexico when tragedy strikes and her family loses everything. As a result, they are forced to migrate to California during the Great Depression of the 1930s and become farmworkers. This excerpt… reveals what life is now like for the story's characters: Esperanza Ortega, who is struggling to adapt to her hardscrabble new life; Hortensia (the Ortega family's housekeeper from Mexico);… and Miguel (Hortensia's son, age seventeen).

Miguel walked in, kissed his mother, then picked up a plate and a fresh *tortilla* and went to the pot of beans. His clothes were covered in mud that had dried gray.

 "How did you get so dirty?"…

 "A group of men showed up from Oklahoma. They said they would work for half the money and the railroad hired all of them…. Some of them have never even worked on a motor before. My boss said that he didn't need me. That they were going to train the new men. He said I could dig ditches or lay tracks if I wanted."…

76

"What did you do?"

 "Can you not tell from my clothes? I dug ditches."…

 "Miguel, how could you agree to such a thing?"…

 "What would you have me do instead? I could have walked out. But I would have no pay for today. Those men from Oklahoma have families, too. We must all work at something or we will all starve."

A temper Esperanza did not recognize raged to the surface. Then, like the irrigation pipes in the fields when the water is first turned on, her anger burst forth.

 "Why didn't your boss tell the others to dig the ditches?!"

She looked at the dough she was holding in her hand and threw it at the wall…. Esperanza's eyes were on fire. She stamped out of the cabin, slamming the door, and walked past the mulberry and the chinaberry trees to the vineyard….

11. ThinkSpeakListen
Why do you think Miguel's behavior made Esperanza angry in this scene?

Miguel eventually caught her arm and pulled her around.

 "What is the matter with you?"

 "Is this the better life that you left Mexico for? Is it? Nothing is right here!… You cannot work on engines because you are Mexican.… We live in a horse stall. And none of this bothers you?"…

 "In Mexico, I was a second-class citizen.… And I would have stayed that way my entire life. At least here, I have a chance, however small, to become more than what I was."…

 "Why don't you go to your boss and confront him? Why don't you speak up for yourself and your talents?"

 "There is more than one way to get what you want in this country. Maybe I must be more determined than others to succeed, but I know that it will happen… Anza, everything will work out."…

 "How do you know these things, Miguel? Do you have some prophecy that I do not?… I can't stand your blind hope. I don't want to hear your optimism about this land of possibility when I see no proof!"

 "As bad as things are, we have to keep trying."

12. ThinkSpeakListen

Compare and contrast Miguel and Esperanza's opinions about life in America, and explain the reasons they use to support their opinions.

Understand Verbs and Verb Phrases: Modal Auxiliaries

 "He said I **could** dig ditches or lay tracks if I wanted."

 "What did you do?"

 "**Can** you not tell from my clothes? I dug ditches."

 "Miguel, how **could** you agree to such a thing?"

 "What **would** you have me do instead? I **could** have walked out. But I **would** have no pay for today. Those men from Oklahoma have families, too. We **must** all work at something or we will all starve."

13. ThinkSpeakListen

Based on what you read in "Asparagus," how would Miguel and Esperanza's lives have been different if they had stayed in Mexico?

British English and Me

Last summer I flew to Great Britain to visit my cousin Fletcher and his family. When they picked me up at the London airport, it was already afternoon, so Fletcher said, "You must be starving. Why don't we go get some grub?"

Visions of grubs—slimy white worms—danced through my head. Who would eat them? Well it turns out that "grub" is British slang for "food."…

At the restaurant, Fletcher took one look at the expression on my face as I read the menu…. "Try the bangers and mash," he encouraged.

Why not? I thought, and was pleased when I received sausages and mashed potatoes.

When we finished, the streets were full of people going to a football match, which is actually soccer in American English. I couldn't believe my good fortune when I found out that Fletcher's parents had purchased tickets!

14. ThinkSpeakListen

Explain the differences between American and British English.

Writing to Sources

In "Asparagus," Esperanza expresses a negative view of the "American Dream," the idea that America is a place of fairness and opportunity for everyone. Do you agree with Esperanza's point of view? In an essay, support your opinion with evidence from "Asparagus," and from at least one other reading from this topic.

Focus of Writing

Type of Writing

Sources You Will Use

Sample Essay

In the story "Asparagus," the main character Esperanza does not believe that America is a place of fairness and opportunity. I disagree with Esperanza's point of view. The experiences of Miguel in "Asparagus" and Annie in "Annie's New Homeland" show that America is still a land where people can change their lives for the better.

Your introduction should introduce the topic, state your opinion, and give the reader a brief idea of what you will write about.

In "Asparagus," Esperanza talks about how unfair things are for Mexicans in America. Miguel then points out that when he was in Mexico, he was treated as a "second-class citizen" there, too. He says that in America, he at least has a chance to make a better life.

Like Miguel, Annie in "Annie's New Homeland" comes to America hoping to improve her life. Annie and her brothers know they will have to work hard, but they look forward to making new lives for themselves in America. This is because America gives people a good chance to improve their lives.

Your body paragraphs should provide logically ordered reasons that are supported by facts and details from the texts.

I agree with Esperanza that America is not perfect. However, I do not agree with her when she says, "Nothing is right here." The examples of Miguel and Annie show that there are a lot of things "right" with America. That is why people still come here from around the world.

Your conclusion should restate your opinion, and provide a closing statement.

81

What value does technology bring to people's lives?

a shipyard

My Language Objectives

- Recognize verb phrases
- Use adverbs to specify frequency
- Use verb tenses to convey various times
- Write a narrative
- Use context clues to understand vocabulary
- Recognize words with Greek and Latin roots

My Content Objectives

- Build vocabulary related to technology and its development
- Expand knowledge of technology's effect on people's lives

a textile factory

a mobile phone

Technology and the Lowell Mill Girls

The following poem, written in 1893, is about an Irish woman who has come to America and is working in a clothing factory in Massachusetts.

A Mill Picture

by Marshall Putnam Thompson

Her wrinkled face is gazing
Through the tangle of the looms,
Where the belts and twisted gearing
Make a network in the rooms.

Does she think of fair Killarney?
Does she dream some old love tune
Is singing through the shuttles
In the mill this afternoon?…

So the superintendent wonders,
As he sees her through the looms,
Where the belts and twisted gearings
Make a network in the rooms.

young woman spinning cotton in a factory, 1908

1. ThinkSpeakListen

Answer the following questions: What do you think the woman in the poem is feeling? What do you think the superintendent is feeling?

Recognize Verb Phrases

	Helping Verb	Main Verb
...an Irish woman who has come to America and **is working** in a clothing factory...	is	working
Her wrinkled face **is gazing**...	is	gazing
Does she **think** of fair Killarney?	Does	think
Does she **dream** some old love tune...	Does	dream
Is singing through the shuttles...	Is	singing

2. ThinkSpeakListen

Explain how verb phrases are formed and when it is necessary to use them.

Eli Whitney's Cotton Gin

by Judi Black

1

Eli Whitney

Eli Whitney was an inventor.... After completing his studies at Yale College, Whitney went to work on a southern cotton plantation....

2

Whitney quickly observed the challenges of processing cotton. Separating the cotton fibers from its seeds was tedious and labor-intensive work....

3

So Whitney developed a machine that separated the seeds from the fibers. He called it a cotton "gin"—short for engine....

4

Two rotating brushes, mounted in a box, pulled the cotton fibers, or lint, through small slots, separating the fiber from the seeds. The brushes were turned by a hand crank....

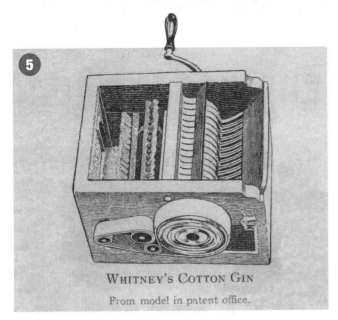

WHITNEY'S COTTON GIN
From model in patent office.

On March 14, 1794, Eli Whitney received a patent for his cotton gin design.... By law, no one else could make this machine.

The invention of the cotton gin led to other developments and changes. The main effect, or impact, was the increase of cotton production.

The demand for cotton in northern factories grew. Farmers realized that, with this efficient machine, they could process more cotton in a harvest and meet the demand....

the Cotton Belt

Farmers began to replace other, less lucrative crops with more cotton. Soon the Cotton Belt was producing more cotton than any other place in the world.

3. ThinkSpeakListen

Answer the following question: Why did many farmers in the Cotton Belt choose to grow cotton rather than other crops?

Lucy Larcom's New England Girlhood

In 1835, when Lucy Larcom was eleven years old, her widowed mother moved her eight children to Lowell, Massachusetts.... Lucy began working at Lowell Mills....

In 1889, she published her autobiography, A New England Girlhood. The work reveals the thoughts and feelings of an observant child about being a mill laborer....

Lucy Larcom

"I never cared much for machinery. The buzzing and hissing and whizzing of pulleys and rollers and spindles and flyers around me often grew tiresome...."

"But in a room below us we were sometimes allowed to peer in through a sort of blind door at the great waterwheel.... It was so huge that we could only watch a few of its spokes at a time...moving with a slow, measured strength through the darkness."

4. ThinkSpeakListen

Answer the following questions: How did Lucy feel about the machines in the mill? How do you think she felt about the waterwheel? Refer to words in the text to support your opinions.

Use <u>Adverbs</u> to Specify Frequency

Sentence	Adverb	Verb the Adverb Modifies
I <u>never</u> <u>cared</u> much for machinery.	<u>never</u>	<u>cared</u>
The buzzing and hissing and whizzing of pulleys and rollers and spindles and flyers around me <u>often</u> <u>grew</u> tiresome.	<u>often</u>	<u>grew</u>
But in a room below us we were <u>sometimes</u> <u>allowed</u> to peer in through a sort of blind door at the great waterwheel.	<u>sometimes</u>	<u>allowed</u>

5. ThinkSpeakListen

Describe one of your favorite hobbies, and use at least two of the adverbs above in your description.

Poems of the Industrial Age

During the Industrial Revolution, many writers reflected on the sea change in technology that was happening around them. Major poets Rudyard Kipling and Carl Sandburg were greatly influenced by the inventions of the Industrial Age they lived in.

The Secret of the Machines

by Rudyard Kipling

Rudyard Kipling

(MODERN MACHINERY)
We were taken from the ore-bed and the mine,
    We were melted in the furnace and the pit—
We were cast and wrought and hammered to design,
    We were cut and filed and tooled and gauged to fit.
Some water, coal, and oil is all we ask,
    And a thousandth of an inch to give us play:
And now, if you will set us to our task,
    We will serve you four and twenty hours a day!…

power looms at
a weaving factory,
Great Britain,
around 1880

90

But remember, please, the Law by which we live,
    We are not built to comprehend a lie,
We can neither love nor pity nor forgive.
    If you make a slip in handling us you die!
We are greater than the Peoples or the Kings—
    Be humble, as you crawl beneath our rods!—
Our touch can alter all created things,
    We are everything on earth—except The Gods!

Though our smoke may hide the Heavens from your eyes,
It will vanish and the stars will shine again,
Because, for all our power and weight and size,
We are nothing more than children of your brain!

cotton mills
in the English
countryside, 1830

6. ThinkSpeakListen

Answer the following question: What do you think this poem is telling us about machines?

Skyscraper

by Carl Sandburg

By day the skyscraper looms in the smoke
and sun and has a soul.
Prairie and valley, streets of the city, pour
people into it and they mingle among its
twenty floors and are poured out again
back to the streets, prairies and valleys.
It is the men and women, boys and girls
so poured in and out all day that give
the building a soul of dreams and
thoughts and memories....

Elevators slide on their cables and tubes
catch letters and parcels and iron pipes
carry gas and water in and sewage out.
Wires climb with secrets, carry light and
carry words, and tell terrors and profits
and loves—curses of men grappling plans
of business and questions of women in
plots of love.

7. ThinkSpeakListen

Answer the following question: What does Sandburg mean when he says the
skyscraper has a soul?

Use Verb Tenses to Convey Various Times

Text	Tense
We <u>were taken</u> from the ore-bed and the mine, We <u>were melted</u> in the furnace and the pit— We <u>were cast</u> and <u>wrought</u> and <u>hammered</u> to design, We <u>were cut</u> and <u>filed</u> and <u>tooled</u> and <u>gauged</u> to fit.	Past
Some water, coal, and oil <u>is</u> all we ask, And a thousandth of an inch to <u>give</u> us play:…	<u>Present</u>
And now, if you <u>will set</u> us to our task, We <u>will serve</u> you four and twenty hours a day!	<u>Future</u>

8. ThinkSpeakListen

Describe the things that you have done today, are doing now, and will do later today. Use past, present, and future verb tenses.

An Adventure to Remember

Last summer, I visited my uncle who lives in New York City. Uncle Harry has always been very literary, so when he left Ohio and moved to New York, it wasn't unexpected. Now he works as an editor for a major publishing company....

He took me to the main observation deck of the Empire State Building, the world's tallest skyscraper.... We rode the elevator up to the eighty-sixth floor (that would have been 1,576 steps). Amazingly, it took less than a minute...

Soon we were on the main deck 1,050 feet above the city streets, peering through high-powered telescopes at spectacular views.

9. ThinkSpeakListen

Describe the photographs of New York that are given above.

Writing to Sources

Writing Prompt

Imagine that you are a skyscraper. Write a narrative about one day in your life. What do you see, hear, think, and feel? Use your imagination as well as inspiration from "The Secret of the Machines" and "Skyscraper" to help you write your narrative.

Purpose for Writing

Focus Question

Sources You Will Use

Sample Narrative

When my windows at the top turn the palest shade of gray, I know it will soon be morning. I begin to listen for the banging of my doors, and the clackety clack of shoes echoing across my cold floors. Mike, as superintendent, makes morning rounds.

> **Setting is established.**
>
> **Details bring the scene to life.**

Mike has been taking care of me since the first day I opened my doors. I watch him watch the workers. I can tell Mike really wants to work on one of the machines. His eyes shine when the factory fills up with workers at every machine.

He watches the workers separate the threads before running them through the power loom. Mike loves to hear that first burst of power. "It's like bringing that machine to life—right?" Mike asks the worker. He wishes he could go home and tell his wife what he made as he sat at one of the machines.

> **Characters are established.**
>
> **Events occur.**

I wish Mike knew that he's the one who brightens my day. Without Mike, I wouldn't stay clean. I'd never feel presentable every morning.

> **The narrator shares interior thoughts and feelings.**

The day passes. My windows at the top start turning golden, and then violet. The sounds slow down. Machines stop with a whir and a clank. Come back tomorrow? I want to ask Mike. You'll come back to me tomorrow, won't you?

> **The conclusion ends the story and gives a closing thought.**

The Making of the Industrial Age

by Kathy Furgang

During the industrial era, new technology allowed different industries to explode. New advancements made some businesses more cost-effective and efficient....

Many of the machines built during the Industrial Revolution were powered by a new technology, the steam engine...

Steam engines for factories, steamboats, and steam locomotives could run anywhere that water and wood or coal fuel was available....

Coal soon became the major fuel source for steam power. Compared with wood, coal yielded more energy, making it more efficient. Coal mining efforts increased....

10. ThinkSpeakListen

Answer the following question: Why, in your opinion, were steamboats and locomotives important to the growth of some industries?

Coal is a nonrenewable resource that is mined, or dug from the ground. Prior to the Industrial Revolution... mining involved digging underground tunnels with pickaxes....

In the 1880s, coal-cutting machines were invented. A series of rotating picks, or a spinning disk, would automatically tear away at thick walls of coal....

The machine was called a continuous miner because it kept the process moving continuously, doing the job of many miners...

Some technology came in the form of new machines. Other technology came from new ways of doing things. Steel is an example...

William Kelly   **Henry Bessemer**

Steel is an extremely strong and ductile metal made from iron and carbon.... Steel was expensive and was used in only a few products, such as knives or swords.

Then in the 1850s, an American named William Kelly and an Englishman named Henry Bessemer both patented processes for mass-producing steel....

An increase in steel productivity made steel less expensive.... The affordability of steel allowed more machines to be manufactured. The mass production of steel also helped launch other industries.

Railroads could be constructed across the nation.... Skyscraping towers more than a thousand feet high could be erected. Eventually, even cars could be built. All of these used steel.

11. ThinkSpeakListen

Answer the following questions: How did the invention of the steam engine affect the coal industry? How did the mass production of steel affect other industries?

Use Context Clues to Understand Vocabulary

Unfamiliar Word	Clues in Nearby Words	Definition
Coal is a nonrenewable resource that is <u>mined</u>, or dug from the ground.	Coal is a nonrenewable resource that is <u>mined</u>, or <u>dug from the ground</u>.	mined: "dug from the ground"
An increase in steel productivity made steel less expensive.... The <u>affordability</u> of steel allowed more machines to be manufactured.	An increase in steel productivity made steel <u>less expensive</u>.... The <u>affordability</u> of steel allowed more machines to be manufactured.	affordability: "acceptable price"
Railroads could be constructed across the nation.... Skyscraping towers more than a thousand feet high could be <u>erected</u>.	Railroads could be <u>constructed</u> across the nation.... Skyscraping <u>towers</u> more than a <u>thousand feet high</u> could be <u>erected</u>.	erected: "built upward"

12. ThinkSpeakListen

Answer the following question: Where in a text can context clues be found?

Samuel Morse: Inventor and Artist

Samuel Morse

Samuel Morse is credited with inventing the electric telegraph and its code of dots and dashes.... However, before becoming an inventor, Morse was an accomplished artist....

In 1825, while working in Washington, D.C., Morse received a letter from his father. The letter, which had taken weeks to arrive, stated that his wife was ill. Morse rushed home, but when he arrived, his wife had already died. Many believe that her death inspired him to create an invention that could send messages quickly and without delay.

In 1832, Morse conceived of the idea of an electric telegraph.... Soon, telegraph wires were built across America and then in countries across the world. Thanks to Samuel Morse, important messages could be sent in seconds, instead of weeks or months.

13. ThinkSpeakListen

Answer the following question: In what ways might the telegraph have changed people's lives?

Recognize Words with Greek and Latin Roots

Text	Roots	
A series of <u>rota</u>ting picks, or a spinning disk, would <u>auto</u>matically tear away at thick walls of coal.	<u>rota</u> – "wheel" <u>autos</u> – "self"	
Samuel Morse is <u>cred</u>ited with inventing the electric telegraph.	<u>credere</u> – "to believe, to trust"	Samuel Morse
In 1832, Morse conceived of the idea of an electric <u>tele</u>graph.	<u>tēle</u> – "far off" <u>graph</u>os – "written"	

14. ThinkSpeakListen

Answer the following questions: How can readers analyze words to discover roots? How can discovering roots help a reader?

Essential Question

What compels us to survive?

rock climbing

My Language Objectives

- Use adjectives to signal states of being
- Expand sentences with adverbs and adverb phrases
- Form adverbs from adjectives
- Combine clauses to connect ideas
- Use sense imagery to describe
- Build research skills

My Content Objectives

- Build vocabulary related to dangers in the natural world
- Understand ways in which people face dangerous situations

dogsledding

a forest fire

Androcles and the Lion
by Aesop

Back in the days of the Roman Empire, a slave named Androcles escaped from his master and then fled into the deep, dark forest. While wandering about in the dense woods, he came upon a lion lying down and loudly moaning and groaning....

As he came near, the lion put out his paw, which was swollen and bleeding. Androcles found that a huge thorn had got into the paw, and that was causing the lion's pain.

Androcles pulled out the thorn and then bound up the paw of the lion. The grateful cat rose and, not unlike a house pet, licked the hand of Androcles.

1. ThinkSpeakListen
Why does Androcles choose to help the lion, rather than run away from it?

104

Use Adjectives to Signal States of Being

meaning:

feeling thankful toward someone

synonyms:

thankful, appreciative

"The **grateful** cat rose and, not unlike a house pet, licked the hand of Androcles."

I was grateful for my brother's help in fixing my car's flat tire.

2. ThinkSpeakListen

Describe both Androcles and the lion, using adjectives to indicate their personalities, attitudes, and moods.

Brushfire! a play excerpt by David Boelke

During "fire season" in Southern California, hot desert winds can blow sparks from wildfires into the bone-dry canyons and valleys of inhabited areas....

Cast of Characters

Ed Acosta: A driven film composer

Meg Acosta: Ed's wife, and mother to Jack and Samantha

Setting

The Acostas' hillside home in Clarita Canyon, a suburb of Los Angeles.... A burning mountain can be seen in the background....

(ED sits at his piano, talking on a cell phone. MEG rushes around, carrying photo albums and boxes.)

ED: I'm telling you, Manny. The opening number is pure gold. Listen. *(He plays a tune.)* What did I tell you?

MEG: Ed, why aren't you loading the car?... The fire department is telling us to evacuate. The Sorensons' place down the hill is already a pile of ashes....

ED: (*Playing another tune into the cell phone*) We're going to need strings here, Manny....

MEG: Ed! I'm seeing a plume of smoke coming from next door. Those flames are moving like race cars! Right at us!

ED: I'll have to get back to you, Manny. (*He hangs up the phone, turns to MEG.*) Why all the drama, Meg? We've survived twenty years of brushfires up here. Now if you'll let me be, fifty musicians are showing up at the studio to record my music tomorrow...9 a.m....sharp!...

MEG: You can feel the heat from the flames! Get whatever matters to you in the van...now!

ED: What matters to me is this piano.

MEG: You're going to put yourself in danger for a beat-up piano? Not me!

3. ThinkSpeakListen

Answer the following question: Why is Ed not paying attention to Meg?

Sinbad and the Valley of Diamonds

Sinbad the Sailor is the hero of Arabian folktales. He undertakes seven voyages. In this installment, Sinbad's ship accidentally left him behind on an island inhabited by a roc, a gigantic legendary bird.... It transports Sinbad to a valley of diamonds.

I had always believed the stories about a valley of diamonds were tall tales. Now, to my amazement, everywhere I looked I saw diamonds! My delight was speedily dampened when I realized the valley was also home to serpents with jaws large enough to swallow a man whole....

I immediately saw an opportunity to escape. After storing several diamonds in my leather bag, I strapped a lump of meat to my back. As I had hoped, an eagle seized the meat and me with it, and flew up to its nest.

4. ThinkSpeakListen

Summarize this story of how Sinbad escapes from a difficult situation.

Expand Sentences with <u>Adverbs</u> and <u>Adverb Phrases</u>

Sentence	Adverbs / Adverb Phrases
	• <u>While wandering about in the dense woods</u>, he came upon a lion lying down and <u>loudly</u> moaning and groaning. • <u>As he came near</u>, the lion put out his paw, which was swollen and bleeding. • The grateful cat rose and, <u>not unlike a house pet</u>, licked the hand of Androcles.
	• My delight was <u>speedily</u> dampened when I realized the valley was also home to serpents with jaws large enough to swallow a man <u>whole</u>. • I <u>immediately</u> saw an opportunity to escape. • <u>As I had hoped</u>, an eagle seized the meat and me with it, and flew up to its nest.

5. ThinkSpeakListen

Explain why an author might want to use adverbs and adverb phrases. How would the above sentences be different without the adverbs and adverb phrases?

The Law of Club and Fang

an excerpt from *The Call of the Wild* by Jack London

During the Alaskan gold rush of the late 1890s, dogs were in demand to pull sleds through the snow. Buck, a new sled dog, has just witnessed a pack of huskies kill another dog, Curly. Now, Francois, the owner of the sled dogs, is giving Buck his first experience pulling a sled with the dog team...

Before he had recovered from the shock caused by the tragic passing of Curly, he received another shock. Francois fastened upon him an arrangement of straps and buckles.

It was a harness, such as he had seen the grooms put on the horses at home.... He hauled Francois on a sled to the forest that fringed the valley....

Though his dignity was sorely hurt by thus being made a draught animal, he was too wise to rebel. He buckled down with a will and did his best.... Francois was stern, demanding instant obedience, and by virtue of his whip receiving instant obedience; while Dave... nipped Buck's hindquarters whenever he was in error.

Spitz was the leader...he growled sharp reproof now and again, or cunningly threw his weight in the traces to jerk Buck into the way he should go. Buck learned easily, and under the combined tuition of his two mates and Francois made remarkable progress.

6. ThinkSpeakListen
Describe Buck's personality, and support your ideas by referring to evidence in the text.

That night Buck faced the great problem of sleeping.... He lay down on the snow and attempted to sleep, but the frost soon drove him shivering to his feet.

Miserable and disconsolate, he wandered about among the many tents, only to find that one place was as cold as another....

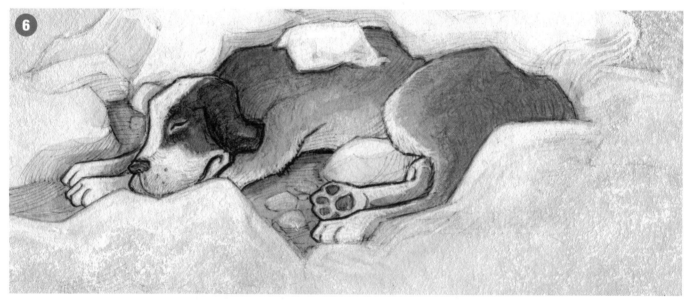

Suddenly the snow gave way beneath his forelegs and he sank down. Something wriggled under his feet.... And there, curled up under the snow in a snug ball, lay Billee....

So that was the way they did it, eh? Buck confidently selected a spot, and...proceeded to dig a hole for himself. In a trice the heat from his body filled the confined space and he was asleep.

7. ThinkSpeakListen

Recount the things that Buck learns over the course of this story.

Form Adverbs from Adjectives

Adjective	Suffix	Example
<u>cunning</u>	-ly	He growled sharp reproof now and again, or **cunningly** threw his weight in the traces to jerk Buck into the way he should go.
<u>easy</u>	-ly	Buck learned **easily**, and under the combined tuition of his two mates and Francois made remarkable progress.

Adjective	Suffix	Example
<u>sudden</u>	-ly	**Suddenly** the snow gave way beneath his forelegs and he sank down.
<u>confident</u>	-ly	Buck **confidently** selected a spot, and… proceeded to dig a hole for himself.

8. ThinkSpeakListen

Answer the following question: What are some other adjectives that can be changed into adverbs by adding the -ly suffix? Use each one in a sentence.

Gold Rush!

Imagine my astonishment when Pa announced that he'd quit his job to go prospecting for gold. At first he intended to leave me behind.... But ever since Ma died, it's been just the two of us. I begged him to take me along and he relented....

A steamship took us north to Alaska. There, by order of the Canadian government, we gathered enough provisions to last us a year. Next, we set off on the Chilkoot Trail into Canada, carrying all our supplies on our backs....

Exhaustion dogged my steps and I nearly gave up. But Pa chivvied me along until at last we reached the Yukon River and prepared to boat downriver to the Klondike and what I hoped would be our golden future.

9. ThinkSpeakListen

Answer the following question: What does the narrator mean by "our golden future"?

Combine Clauses to Connect Ideas

Connecting Word	Type of Relationship Indicated
<u>Before</u> he had recovered from the shock caused by the tragic passing of Curly, he received another shock.	<u>Sequence</u>
<u>Though</u> his dignity was sorely hurt by thus being made a draught animal, he was too wise to rebel.	<u>Contrast</u>
He lay down on the snow and attempted to sleep, <u>but</u> the frost soon drove him shivering to his feet.	<u>Contrast</u>
Suddenly the snow gave way beneath his forelegs <u>and</u> he sank down.	<u>Result</u>
I begged him to take me along <u>and</u> he relented.	<u>Result</u>
But Pa chivvied me along <u>until</u> at last we reached the Yukon River…	<u>Duration</u>

10. ThinkSpeakListen

Describe some of the hardships that you think Klondike gold miners faced. Use some of the connecting words given above.

Julie Fights for Survival

an excerpt from *Julie of the Wolves* by Jean Craighead George

Thirteen-year-old Julie, known as Miyax in her Eskimo village, has run away from an arranged marriage. She ends up lost in the Alaskan wilderness, where she learns to survive by observing, befriending, and finally becoming accepted by a pack of wolves.

As she waited for sleep she listened to the polar wind whistle, and the dry grasses whined like the voice of the old bent lady.

"Jello!"[1] she screamed, sitting bolt upright. He was almost beside her, his teeth bared as he growled. Then he picked up her pack and ran.

1 Jello—a lone wolf that has tried to join the pack

11. ThinkSpeakListen

Answer the following question: Why do you think Jello stole Julie's pack?

She jumped out of bed and started after him, for her very life was in that pack—food, needles, knives, even her boots....

She could go nowhere without boots; nor could she make new ones. Her needles and ulo,[2] the tools of survival, were all in the pack. Shivering, she slid into bed and cried....

When she opened her eyes it was daylight.... She smelled something sweet and recognized the scent of wolf urine.... Someone had greeted her during the night. It could not have been Jello for the scent did not have the bitter odor of an angry and desolate wolf.... It must have been Amaroq.[3]...

2 ulo—a half-moon-shaped knife used primarily by Eskimo women

3 Amaroq—the wolf-pack leader

Its light and loving scent gave her a sense of security and she smiled at the sun....

Wrapping the drag around one foot and her sleeping skin around the other, she clomped awkwardly through the grass...hoping that Jello, having eaten her meat, would have abandoned the pack.

She did not care about the food anymore. Her ulo and needles and matches were more important to find. With them she could make shoes, hunt, and cook....

"Ayi!" she gasped. On the side of a ground swell lay Jello, his body torn in bloody shreds, his face contorted. Beside him lay her backpack!

12. ThinkSpeakListen

Explain how Julie's emotions change over the course of this story. Point to evidence in the text to support your ideas.

Use Sense Imagery to Describe

Description	Sense
As she waited for sleep she listened to the polar wind **whistle**, and the dry grasses **whined** like the voice of the old bent lady.	sound
Shivering, she slid into bed and cried.	touch
She smelled something **sweet** and recognized the scent of wolf urine.... It could not have been Jello for the scent did not have the **bitter odor** of an angry and desolate wolf.	smell
On the side of a ground swell lay Jello, his body **torn in bloody shreds**, his face **contorted**.	sight

13. ThinkSpeakListen

Recount what you have done so far today, using sense imagery in your descriptions.

119

Survival in the Arctic

In 2003, explorer Pen Hadow became the first person to trek 770 kilometers (478 miles) solo from Canada to the Geographic North Pole.... Would you like to take on such a far-flung adventure? Here is Hadow's advice to ensure your well-being.

1. Wear at least four layers of warm, breathable clothing....

2. Take a sleeping bag designed for extreme cold....

3. Watch for symptoms of frostbite. Extreme cold turns your skin chalky white due to tissue damage....

4. Keep your body fueled with meals and snacks that are high in calories....

5. Travel with someone. You will be able to watch out for each other.

6. Finally, if you encounter a polar bear, don't panic. A bright, loud flare should frighten it off.

14. ThinkSpeakListen

Answer the following question: Aside from the things that Hadow lists, what would you want to bring with you to the North Pole? Explain why you would choose those things.

Building Research Skills

Writing Prompt

At the end of "Julie Fights for Survival," Julie seems confident that she'll be able to survive the Arctic winter with what's in her backpack. Do you agree or disagree? Imagine that you have been asked to answer this question in an opinion essay. As a guiding question, ask yourself: What are conditions like in the Arctic during the winter? Read and take notes from at least two sources to help you answer this question. List the sources of your information.

Purpose for Writing

Type of Writing

Guiding Question

Sources You Will Use

Take Notes: Use Direct Quotes to Avoid Plagiarism

Original Text	Quotations
In the Arctic, winter temperatures can drop as low as –40°F. The sun is low in the sky even at noon, and days are short. In some places, the sun does not rise for months. This is called polar night.	According to one source, "The sun is low in the sky even at noon, and days are short."
	Some areas even fall into a "polar night," during which the sun is never seen.
Precipitation during an Arctic winter can range from 8 inches to 20 inches, and when winds reach top speeds, whiteout conditions can occur. During a whiteout, snowfall partially or completely blocks a person's view of the surroundings.	A blizzard in the Arctic can cause a "whiteout," as "snowfall partially or completely blocks a person's view of the surroundings."

Paragraph+

Conditions during an Arctic winter are harsh. According to one source, "The sun is low in the sky even at noon, and days are short." Some areas even fall into a "polar night," during which the sun is never seen. In addition, as much as 20 inches of precipitation can fall. A blizzard in the Arctic can cause a "whiteout," as "snowfall partially or completely blocks a person's view of the surroundings."

Essential Question

How does conflict shape a society?

a Revolutionary War battle

My Language Objectives

- Understand the language of sequence
- Form and use irregular verbs
- Use adverbials to add details about time
- Use conjunctions to connect ideas
- Understand and use figurative language: similes
- Write a journal entry

My Content Objectives

- Build vocabulary related to the Revolutionary War
- Understand how conflict shapes society

Civil War soldiers

U.S. soldiers today

123

Yankee Doodle Boy

excerpts from *The Diary of Private Joseph Plumb Martin*
by Joseph Plumb Martin

It was the year 1776, and the thirteen American colonies had declared their independence from Great Britain. Joseph Plumb Martin was just fifteen years old... In the excerpts below, he tells of the British surrender at the Battle of Yorktown in 1781.

Soon after landing we marched to Williamsburg...and very soon after... we prepared to move down...

About noon the much-wished-for signal went up....

We arrived at the trenches a little before sunset.... I then concluded we were about to make a general assault...before dark I was informed of the whole plan...

Before night we were informed that the British had surrendered and that the siege was ended.

1. ThinkSpeakListen
How does the structure of this text affect your understanding of the topic?

Understand the Language of Sequence

<u>Soon after landing</u> we marched to Williamsburg...and <u>very soon after</u>... we prepared to move down.

<u>About noon</u> the much-wished-for signal went up.

We arrived at the trenches <u>a little before sunset</u>.

...<u>before dark</u> I was informed of the whole plan.

<u>Before night</u> we were informed that the British had surrendered and that the siege was ended.

2. ThinkSpeakListen

Use the language of sequence to recount what happened to Joseph Plumb Martin during the Battle of Yorktown in 1781.

Road to Revolution

by Susan Buckley

For 150 years Great Britain's thirteen American colonies had had time to grow… the colonists still thought of themselves as British citizens. But… also thought of themselves as Americans….

The British saw them as an economic resource. The colonists' duty was to supply resources such as sugar and tobacco to Britain and to buy British goods….

Anger Builds

All of this changed in the 1760s, after the French and Indian War. Defending the colonies in that war had cost the British a great deal….

The colonists began to rebel…. they formed committees such as the Sons of Liberty and the Daughters of Liberty.

To Fight or Not?

In 1769, George Washington expressed his hope that the colonies could avoid military action.... George Washington favored commercial actions such as boycotting, or refusing to buy, British goods....

The fighting began in Massachusetts, which was a hotbed of rebellion from the beginning. The first casualties were in Boston when British soldiers fired on a group of colonists. Patriots called it the "Boston Massacre."

Declaring Independence

Patrick Henry took a very different position.... In a speech...he said: *The war is inevitable—and let it come! ...there is no peace. The war is actually begun! ...give me liberty or give me death!...*

In July 1776, the American colonies demanded their independence from Great Britain. They declared themselves "free and independent states," the United States of America.

3. ThinkSpeakListen

Compare and contrast the positions George Washington and Patrick Henry held in the fight for independence. How were they alike? How were they different?

Deborah Sampson, Revolutionary Soldier

Deborah Sampson was born in 1760. The daughter of poor parents, she worked as a servant and a teacher before deciding to join the fight for independence. Sampson knew that she would not be accepted on the battlefield as a woman, so she hid her identity and disguised herself as a man....

Sampson performed bravely in battle. She survived a sword wound and a musket shot... When Sampson was put in the hospital for a fever, one of the doctors discovered that the soldier named Robert Shurtleff was really a woman!

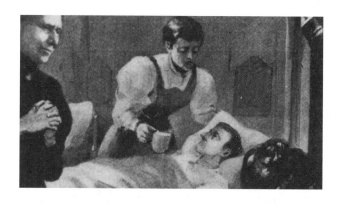

Deborah Sampson received an honorable discharge from the army in 1783. After returning home from service, she became one of America's first female lecturers.... Sampson died in 1827 and was buried near her home in Massachusetts. In 1983, Sampson was named the official heroine of the Commonwealth of Massachusetts.

4. ThinkSpeakListen

Explain how Deborah Sampson joined the fight for independence.

Form and Use Irregular Verbs

Example from Texts	Present Tense	Past Tense
Sampson <u>knew</u> that she would not be accepted on the battlefield as a woman…	know	knew
…so she <u>hid</u> her identity and disguised herself as a man.	hide	hid
When Sampson was <u>put</u> in the hospital for a fever…	put	put
…one of the doctors discovered that the soldier named Robert Shurtleff <u>was</u> really a woman!	is	was
After returning home from service, she <u>became</u> one of America's first female lecturers.	become	became

5. ThinkSpeakListen

Use irregular verbs to describe how Deborah Sampson became a soldier in the fight for independence.

The Nation at War

by Susan Buckley

The United States was born in the victory of the American Revolution.... Almost eighty years later Americans fought another long and bloody war to determine whether they would remain one nation or divide into two.

Voices of War

One young soldier described...a Civil War battle in 1861: ...*it was a sad and dreary day.... I had to be up all night to guard the wounded—it was the saddest thing I ever saw to hear the moans of the wounded and dying....*

Less than a century later, another young American soldier described his feelings in World War II: ...*It makes you feel mighty small, helpless, and alone... Without faith, I don't see how anyone could stand this.*

Fighting for Independence: The American Revolution

"We have it in our power, to begin the world over again... the birthday of a new world is at hand," wrote Thomas Paine.... he argued that independence from Britain was the only sensible route for Americans to take....

The fighting lasted for six years. The Americans were greatly outnumbered: About 2.5 million people lived in the thirteen colonies, while there were about 7.5 million inhabitants of Great Britain....

At first, most soldiers fought with local or state militias. Militias are groups of "regular" citizens who join together for a short time. Many served...for only six months and then returned home.

At the same time, though, General George Washington created a real army, the Continental Army. It was made up of soldiers from all thirteen colonies....

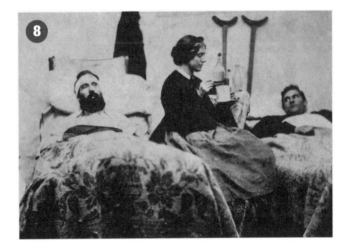

Women like Abigail Adams used their influence to support the Patriot cause. Some women, such as Deborah Sampson and Molly Pitcher, found ways to fight on the battlefield....

6. ThinkSpeakListen
What are some ways members of the colonies helped the war effort?

One Nation Indivisible?: The Civil War

In the bloodiest war of our history, the United States fought to keep its unity as a nation.... The two sides... held conflicting beliefs. Issues of slavery and states' rights were at the core of the dispute....

After Abraham Lincoln was elected president of the United States, eleven Southern states left the Union and declared themselves a separate nation. They called it the Confederate States of America, or the Confederacy....

At War in Other Lands

The last war fought...in U.S. territory was the Civil War.... from the twentieth century to the present time, the nation has been involved in wars around the world.

The United States has brought its power to end colonialism... The nation has joined allies defending freedom... fought Communist forces... and... brave American soldiers are fighting for freedom around the world.

7. ThinkSpeakListen

What are some of the reasons the United States has gone to war?

Use Adverbials to Add Details About Time

Almost eighty years later Americans fought another long and bloody war to determine whether they would remain one nation or divide into two.

Less than a century later, another young American soldier described his feelings in World War II…

After Abraham Lincoln was elected president of the United states, eleven Southern states left the Union…

From the twentieth century to the present time, the nation has been involved in wars around the world.

8. ThinkSpeakListen
Use adverbials to describe how these wars have changed society.

Two Letters from Boston, Massachusetts—1775

My Dear Sister,   June 10, 1775

I have settled in at the army camp, and for the most part I am faring well.

One thing that troubles me...is the threat of camp fever. This deadly fever is brought on by a lack of cleanliness. Although I...remain clean...many others do not....

Please give my love to Mother....

Your brother, Robert

Dearest Mary,   July 30, 1775

The General has instructed that we place ornamental ribbons on our hats....

And what of the regular soldiers?... One soldier may wear a heavy coat and a straw hat, while another dresses in moccasins and tattered britches. Yet despite this, we are united in spirit as we get ready to fight....

I will say goodnight now, Mary. I think of you and little Sarah each day and recollect our happy times together....

Your husband, John

9. ThinkSpeakListen

Compare Robert's and John's feelings about the war. How are they the same? How are they different?

Use Conjunctions to Connect Ideas

Conjunctions		
I have settled in at the army camp. For the most part I am faring well.	**and**	I have settled in at the army camp, and for the most part I am faring well.
The General has instructed We place ornamental ribbons on our hats.	**that**	The General has instructed that we place ornamental ribbons on our hats.
One soldier may wear a heavy coat and a straw hat. Another dresses in moccasins and tattered britches.	**while**	One soldier may wear a heavy coat and a straw hat, while another dresses in moccasins and tattered britches.
Yet despite this, we are united in spirit. We get ready to fight.	**as**	Yet despite this, we are united in spirit as we get ready to fight.

10. ThinkSpeakListen

Based on your reading and your understanding of conjunctions, write a sentence using the conjunction "while."

135

The Youth in Battle

an excerpt from *The Red Badge of Courage* by Stephen Crane

The classic Civil War novel The Red Badge of Courage *(1895) is praised for its realistic depiction of war and the emotional impact on soldiers.... In the following excerpt from Chapter 5, a young soldier finally experiences battle after a lengthy wait.*

Across the smoke-infested fields came a brown swarm of running men who were giving shrill yells. They came on, stooping and swinging their rifles at all angles. A flag, tilted forward, sped near the front.

As he caught sight of them the youth was momentarily startled by a thought that perhaps his gun was not loaded. He stood trying to rally his faltering intellect so that he might recollect the moment when he had loaded, but he could not....

The captain of the company had been pacing excitedly to and fro in the rear…. "Reserve your fire, boys—don't shoot till I tell you—save your fire—wait till they get close up…"

Perspiration streamed down the youth's face, which was soiled like that of a weeping urchin. He frequently, with a nervous movement, wiped his eyes with his coat sleeve….

He got the one glance at the foe-swarming field in front of him, and instantly ceased to debate the question of his piece being loaded.

Before he was ready to begin—before he had announced to himself that he was about to fight—he threw the obedient well-balanced rifle into position and fired a first wild shot….

11. ThinkSpeakListen

Think of a time when you were very nervous. Use descriptive language to explain what that experience was like.

The regiment was like a firework that, once ignited, proceeds superior to circumstances until its blazing vitality fades.

It wheezed and banged with a mighty power. He pictured the ground before it as strewn with the discomfited.

There was a consciousness always of the presence of his comrades about him. He felt the subtle battle brotherhood more potent even than the cause for which they were fighting....

Presently he began to feel the effects of the war atmosphere—a blistering sweat, a sensation that his eyeballs were about to crack like hot stones. A burning roar filled his ears.

12. ThinkSpeakListen

How do you think the narrator of "The Youth in Battle" feels about the experience of being in a battle?

Understand and Use Figurative Language: <u>Similes</u>

Perspiration streamed down the youth's face, which was soiled <u>like that of a weeping urchin.</u>	
The regiment was <u>like a firework that, once ignited,</u> proceeds superior to circumstances until its blazing vitality fades.	
Presently he began to feel the effects of the war atmosphere—a blistering sweat, a sensation that his eyeballs were about to crack <u>like hot stones.</u>	

13. ThinkSpeakListen

Refer back to the activity on page 137. Use similes to improve your description of what it is like to be nervous.

Young Patriots

In 1776, young Joseph Plumb Martin knew he wanted to join the army... Although he was only fifteen, he... first joined a state militia. Then he enlisted in the Continental Army. Joseph served as a Continental soldier through almost the whole war....

Sybil Ludington was a teenager whose father was the colonel of a local militia.... Colonel Ludington needed to muster his troops.... Sybil jumped on a horse and rode miles through the night to alert the men....

Bravery was also a necessity for any young man who accepted the assignment of Revolutionary War drummer. A drummer's duty was to beat out rhythms to help direct troops during battle. A sure sign of a drummer's courage was his ability to play while bullets flew around him.... These young musicians... provided a marching beat and boosted morale.

14. ThinkSpeakListen

Use adverbials and similes to describe a day for a young patriot. Use conjunctions to connect your ideas.

Writing to Sources

Writing Prompt

Imagine that you are a soldier in the Union Army. Write a journal entry describing your thoughts before a large battle. Use firsthand accounts of soldiers' experiences from the primary sources in "Yankee Doodle Boy" and "The Nation at War," facts about the Civil War from the informational text in "The Nation at War," and details from "The Youth in Battle" as the inspiration for your writing.

Focus of Writing

Type of Writing

Sources You Will Use

Sample Journal Entry

I could hear artillery pounding the fields with a thundering noise. From our Union Army camp, I could hear federal cannons fire at the Confederate base, and gun smoke violently filled the air. My eyes filled with tears from the smoke, while my ears filled with sobbing prayers from a Union Army soldier kneeling beside me. This is how all battles begin: with cannons firing and soldiers praying. I came all the way from New York City to Gettysburg, Pennsylvania. I'm not sure if I will make it back in one piece.

Establish the situation.

Right then and there, I heard our captain cry: "Company, load your weapons!" We lifted our bodies from the dirt and gathered our rifles. I placed the butt of my rifled musket on the ground between my feet, poured the gunpowder into the barrel, and rammed the bullet down the muzzle of my gun. My hands were wet with sweat. The rifle slipped from my fingers and fell to the grass.

Develop events by describing actions, thoughts, and feelings. Show how characters respond to situations.

While reaching for my gun, I felt my pendant dangling around my neck, the same pendant that my mother had sent me three months earlier, and perhaps the only thing that might keep me alive.

Provide a sense of closure.

Essential Question

What does water mean to people and the societies they live in?

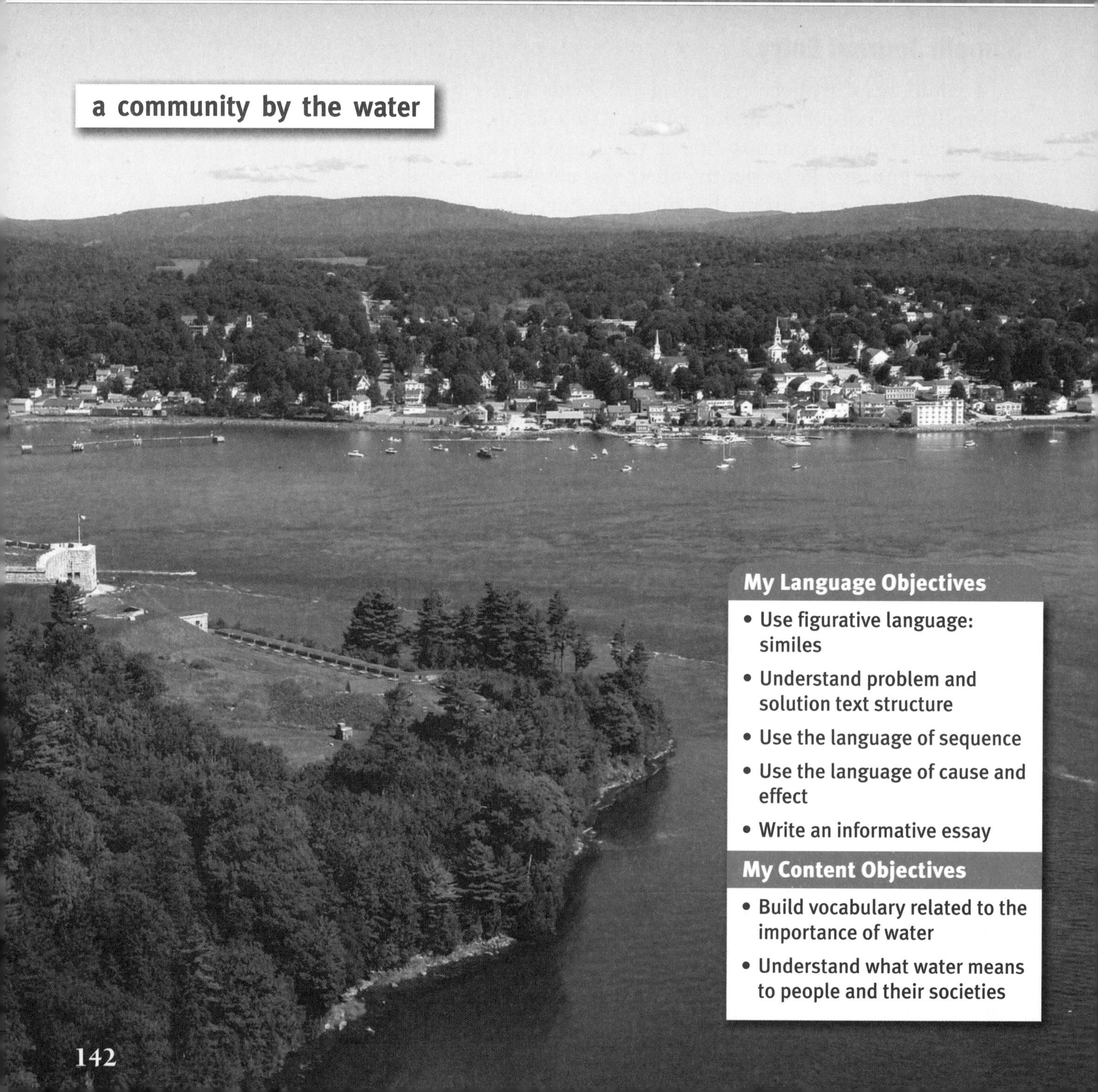

a community by the water

My Language Objectives

- Use figurative language: similes
- Understand problem and solution text structure
- Use the language of sequence
- Use the language of cause and effect
- Write an informative essay

My Content Objectives

- Build vocabulary related to the importance of water
- Understand what water means to people and their societies

fishing in a river

a dry landscape

143

The Water Famine

a Native American Legend retold by Gare Thompson

A long, long time ago, a mean Monster Bullfrog controlled the river. He forbade the people from using its waters, which turned fatal for some who died of thirst. The people called on their Spirit Chief, Gluskabe, to help them.... "The Monster Frog is killing us..." they said in weakened voices. Their voices were as dry and parched as brush in high summer....

As fast as a bee taking nectar, Gluskabe grabbed the Monster Bullfrog and pushed down his back.... Gluskabe took an axe and cut down a large yellow birch tree. When it fell down, the yellow birch tree obliterated the Monster Bullfrog.

The water from the river flowed over the many branches of the yellow birch tree. And that is how the Penobscot river originated.... The water famine was ended forever.

1. ThinkSpeakListen
Summarize "The Water Famine" in your own words.

Use Figurative Language: Similes

Simile	Comparison	
Their throats were as dry and parched as brush in high summer.	**throats** dry, parched summer brush	
As fast as a bee taking nectar…	**Gluskabe's speed** the speed of a bee quickly taking nectar	

2. ThinkSpeakListen

Why do you think the similes in this legend use things found in nature?

Water-Wise Landscaper

a Climate Kids interview with Michelle Pekko-Seymoure

Michelle Pekko-Seymoure

Michelle Pekko-Seymoure is a landscape designer...who specializes in creating natural environments in desert areas.

A desert is a type of habitat that typically gets less than twenty inches of rainfall a year.... Therefore, Michelle plans gardens in ways that use as little water as possible.

Climate Kids...conducted the following interview.

Climate Kids: Michelle, why should people care how much water they use on their yards or gardens?

Michelle: In many regions, water is scarce. Some cities covered in green lawns and spouting fountains are actually in the middle of dry deserts with little rainfall.

CK: But we don't need rain. We can turn on the sprinklers and give our pretty lawns as much water as they need. Right?

Michelle: No. In order to live in these places, people have to dig deep wells to find water. Or they have to pipe water in from lakes or reservoirs.... They need to conserve water so they don't run out completely....

CK: So...I guess we should all just let our lawns turn brown.

Michelle: Not at all! That's the great thing about xeriscaping.

CK: Zer-i-what's-it?

Michelle: Xeriscaping is the creation of beautiful, natural-looking landscapes that need very little water.

3. ThinkSpeakListen

Why do some people like to have lawns and gardens?

Pecos Bill and the Tornado

Pecos Bill was the roughest, toughest cowboy in the West....

Back then, the West was in the middle of a terrible drought. In fact, the area was so devoid of moisture, livestock were dehydrating and blowing around like big brown tumbleweeds!

So when a ferocious tornado rumbled into the area, Bill jumped at the opportunity to end the drought....

Bill grabbed his lasso, roped the rotating spout, and hoisted himself onto it with a joyful whoop.... As Bill rode the tornado across Texas, New Mexico, and Arizona, he used his powerful hands to squeeze water from it.

The water showered down on the parched soil and everyone cheered. Finally the tornado ran out of steam and dumped Bill in California. But when Bill fell from the sky, he hit the ground so hard he made an enormous dent. Today we call that great depression Death Valley.

4. ThinkSpeakListen

How are the stories of Gluskabe and of Pecos Bill similar? How are they different?

Understand Problem and Solution Text Structure

Text	Problem	Solution
The Water Famine	The Monster Frog "forbade the people from using its waters, which turned fatal for some who died of thirst."	"The people called on their Spirit Chief, Gluskabe, to help them."
Water-Wise Landscaper	"In many regions, water is scarce. Some cities covered in green lawns and spouting fountains are actually in the middle of dry deserts with little rainfall."	"Xeriscaping is the creation of beautiful, natural-looking landscapes that need very little water."
Pecos Bill and the Tornado	"…the West was in the middle of a terrible drought."	"As Bill rode the tornado across Texas, New Mexico, and Arizona, he used his powerful hands to squeeze water from it."

5. ThinkSpeakListen

How else might Pecos Bill have solved the drought?

The Pagoda on the Hill of Imperial Springs

an excerpt from *Myths and Legends of China* by E. T. C. Werner

In the new city of Peking, a sudden and untoward event occurred that spread dismay.... One day when the Prince of Yen went into the hall of audience, one of his ministers reported that "the wells are thirsty and the rivers dried up." There was no water, and the people were all in the greatest alarm....

It is necessary to explain the cause of this scarcity of water. There was a dragon's cave outside the east gate of the city.... In digging out the earth to build a wall for the new city some workmen had broken into this dragon's cave.... The dragon was exceedingly angry. He became determined to shift his abode, but the she-dragon said: "We have lived here thousands of years, and shall we suffer the Prince of Yen to drive us forth thus? If we do go, we will collect all the water and place it into our yin-yang baskets.

"And at midnight we will appear in a dream to the Prince. In the dream, we will request permission to retire. If he gives us permission to do so, and allows us also to take our baskets of water with us, he will fall into our trap...."

The two dragons then transformed themselves into an old man and an old woman...and appeared to him in a dream....

The Prince readily assented, little dreaming of the danger he was incurring.

The dragons were highly delighted. They immediately hastened out of his presence. Then they filled the baskets with all the water there was in Peking. Finally, they carried the baskets of water off with them.

6. ThinkSpeakListen

Recount the events of this story so far. Remember to tell the story with the correct sequence of events.

When the Prince awoke...he discovered that his dream-visitors had been dragons, who had taken the waters of Peking.... In haste the Prince donned his armor. Then he mounted his black steed.... He pressed on his horse, which went swift as the wind...till he came up with the water-stealing dragons.... He thrust his spear into one of the baskets. It made a great hole, out of which the water rushed so rapidly that the Prince...dashed off at full speed to save himself....

On galloped the Prince, followed by the roaring water, till he reached a hill.... When he gained the top he found that it stood out of the water like an island, completely surrounded.... In the center was a fountain.... From the midst of this there arose a pagoda....

When the Prince returned to the city, he was hailed as its savior.... Since that time, Peking has never had the misfortune to be without water.

7. ThinkSpeakListen

What is the main problem in this story? How does the Prince solve the problem?

Use the Language of Sequence

In digging out the earth to build a wall for the new city some workmen had broken into this dragon's cave.

"And **at midnight** we will appear in a dream to the Prince."

The two dragons **then** transformed themselves into an old man and an old woman.

They **immediately** hastened out of his presence.

When the Prince awoke…he discovered that his dream-visitors had been dragons, who had taken the waters of Peking.

On galloped the Prince, followed by the roaring water, **till** he reached a hill…

When the Prince returned to the city, he was hailed as its savior.

8. ThinkSpeakListen
Recount the events of this story, using sequence terms other than the ones above.

Why the Ocean Has Tides

Raven and his people...searched for seafood on the shore. They never ventured into the water for their food, however, because the ocean was too deep.... One night in a dream, Raven visualized a woman who controlled the ocean level.... "If I can persuade her to release the line," Raven thought, "the Big Water will recede and we can gather more seafood!"

So Raven flew to the end of the world.... He found her inside a cave, holding the tide line securely across her lap....

Clever Raven proceeded to mumble to himself outside the cave.... When the woman leaned forward to hear what Raven was saying, he kicked up sand. The woman could not see momentarily and she dropped the line.

"You've outsmarted me," the woman exclaimed.... "Now the Big Water has dropped so low, all the ocean creatures will soon die. Then your people will have no seafood at all. But if you help me clear the sand from my eyes, I will agree to control the water in a uniform way."

9. ThinkSpeakListen
Describe the problem and solution in this story.

Research and Writing

Writing Prompt

Earth's water supply is endangered by many factors, such as pollution, overconsumption, and climate change. Research one of these threats, and write an informational essay about how people are responding to the threat.

Background Information

Type of Writing

Purpose of Writing

Water Safety Threats	Effects on Water Supply	Ways People Are Responding
pollution	harms aquatic life	seeking government regulation
overconsumption	threat to fish population	recommending self-regulation by fisheries
climate change	makes some ocean areas unfit for certain aquatic species	finding ways to reduce the CO_2 emissions created by fossil fuels

Questions and Answers About the Oceans

a Climate Kids article

Question #1: Why is the ocean important?

Our world is a water world, and the ocean covers 70 percent of Earth's surface.... The ocean contains about 97 percent of all the water on Earth.

The ocean plays a starring role in whatever happens with the environment. One big part of its role is to soak up energy (heat) and distribute it more evenly around Earth. Another part is to soak up carbon dioxide, or CO_2.

Question #2: How does the ocean soak up energy?

The ocean does an excellent job of absorbing excess heat from the atmosphere. The top few meters of the ocean store as much heat as Earth's entire atmosphere.

So, as the planet warms, it's the ocean that gets most of the extra energy. But if the ocean gets too warm, then the plants and animals that live in it must adapt—or die.

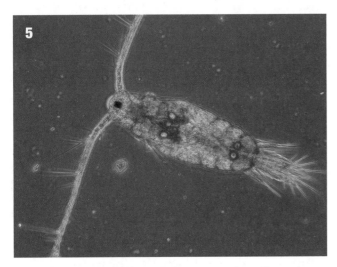

Algae and plankton are at the bottom of the food chain. Plankton includes many different kinds of tiny animals, plants, and bacteria that just float and drift in the ocean.

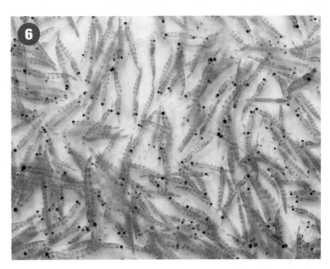

Other tiny animals such as krill—sort of like little shrimp—eat the plankton. Fish, and even whales and seals, feed on the krill.

In some parts of the ocean, krill populations have dropped by more than 80 percent. Why? Krill like to breed in really cold water near sea ice.

What would happen if there were no sea ice? What would happen if there were very little plankton or krill? The whole food web could come unraveled....

10. ThinkSpeakListen

Explain how a drop in the krill population can cause problems for the ocean's food web. How is this related to the warming of Earth?

Question #3: How does the ocean soak up CO_2?

Fish and other animals in the ocean breathe oxygen and give off carbon dioxide (CO_2), just like land animals. Ocean plants take in the carbon dioxide and give off oxygen, just like land plants.

The ocean is great at sucking up CO_2 from the air. It absorbs about one-quarter of the CO_2 that we humans create when we burn fossil fuels (oil, coal, and natural gas)....

However, the ocean and everything in it are paying a price. The ocean is becoming more acidic. What does this mean? Liquids are either acid or alkaline....

The alkalinity of the ocean is very important in maintaining a delicate balance needed for animals...to make protective shells. If the water is too acidic, the animals may not be able to make strong shells.

11. ThinkSpeakListen

What is one effect of too much carbon dioxide in the ocean?

Use the Language of Cause and Effect

Cause	Effect
But if the ocean gets too warm,	then the plants and animals that live in it must adapt—or die.
What would happen if there were very little plankton or krill?	The whole food web could come unraveled.
The ocean is becoming more acidic. What does this mean?…	If the water is too acidic, the animals may not be able to make strong shells.

12. ThinkSpeakListen

Explain what might happen if the ocean's food web is disturbed.

The Great Barrier Reef

Off the northeastern coast of Australia lies one of the largest natural wonders of the world. Big enough to be seen from space, the Great Barrier Reef is…an expansive complex of many reefs, islands, and sandy shoals. Hundreds of different types of corals make up the Great Barrier Reef, and the diversity of marine life is impressive.…

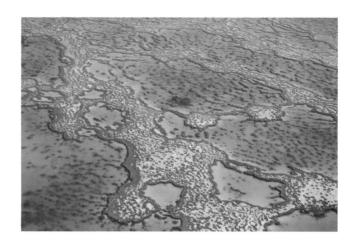

But there is a problem.… As our climate changes and global temperatures rise, corals in the Great Barrier Reef are at risk. Coral polyps are dependent upon algae for food. When the water around a coral reef gets too warm, it affects the algae. In turn, the coral is affected. Coral bleaching takes place.…

Most corals can recover, yet scientists…are confident that there is a link between climate change and coral bleaching. They also know that the effects of coral bleaching are cumulative.…

The Great Barrier Reef is truly one of the world's greatest natural treasures.

13. ThinkSpeakListen

In your opinion, is it important for us to try to save the Great Barrier Reef? Why or why not?

Research and Writing

Sample Opinion Essay

The overfishing of the oceans is a serious problem. Some kinds of fish, such as cod, have been fished almost to extinction. Some scientists think that if we do not regulate fishing, there may be no fish left in the sea by 2050.

The topic of the essay is introduced.

Studies by the Wildlife Conservation Society have shown how difficult it is to solve the problem of overfishing. "In an age when fisheries around the world are collapsing, fisheries experts have struggled to find the magic balance between livelihoods and conservation," says Dr. Tim McClanahan. He is the head of the Wildlife Conservation Society's coral reef research and conservation program.

One study found that it was important for fishing communities to come up with their own rules. These rules are necessary for sustainable ocean fishing. When the people who do the fishing create the rules, the rules are more likely to be followed.

The topic is developed with facts, details, and quotes.

Overfishing is a big problem, but experts believe that fishing communities themselves might be able to solve the problem and make sure there are enough fish in the sea.

The concluding statement summarizes the information presented in the essay.

How do economic changes impact societies?

a crowded city street

My Language Objectives

- Use noun phrases to add detail
- Use irregular nouns
- Combine clauses to condense ideas
- Use introductory prepositional phrases to establish time
- Write a narrative

My Content Objectives

- Build vocabulary related to economic change
- Describe how economic changes influence people's lives

a suspension bridge

a city block

The Founding of Chicago

by Vaughn Smith

Native Americans have lived in the Chicago region of Illinois for thousands of years. The area served as home and as a trade center for different tribes...

One tribe...is known as Mound Builders. They built huge mounds of earth, which they used as burial grounds and centers for religious ceremonies...

Jacques Marquette
Louis Jolliet

The first Europeans to discover the Chicago area were Louis Jolliet and Jacques Marquette in 1673. Jolliet was a French Canadian explorer; Marquette was a Jesuit missionary....

Jean Baptiste Point du Sable

The first settler of Chicago was Jean Baptiste Point du Sable...a free black man believed to have been born in Haiti or Santo Domingo. He settled in Chicago around the late 1770s or early 1780s.

1. ThinkSpeakListen

Summarize the events described in this text.

164

Use Noun Phrases to Add Detail

Sentence	Subject	Linking Verb	Noun Phrase
The first Europeans to discover the Chicago area were Louis Jolliet and Jacques Marquette in 1673.	The first Europeans to discover the Chicago area	were	Louis Jolliet and Jacques Marquette
Jolliet was a French Canadian explorer…	Jolliet	was	French Canadian explorer
Marquette was a Jesuit missionary.	Marquette	was	Jesuit missionary
The first settler of Chicago was Jean Baptiste Point du Sable.	The first settler of Chicago	was	Jean Baptiste Point du Sable

2. ThinkSpeakListen

How do noun phrases give readers information?

Chicago: An American Hub

by Ena Kao

Chicago began as a settlement on a river and quickly grew into an important and prosperous city....

People flocked to this new city, searching for jobs and hoping for a better life. Many of these new residents were immigrants from Europe.

People worked in factories that produced meat and tools, while others worked on the railroads....

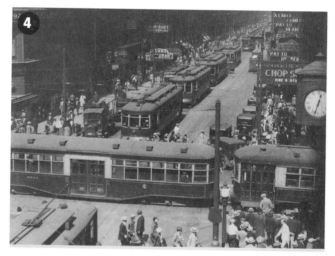

Chicago soon became one of the largest cities in the United States. According to the U.S. Census of 1870, nearly 300,000 people called Chicago home.

Chicago today is a vibrant city that continues to grow, change, and attract people and new businesses.

Nearly three million people and more than 400 major corporations call Chicago home.

It is also a leader in sustainable business, leading the "green" economy.

The city continues to draw new immigrants to its hub, and its population has become increasingly diverse.

3. ThinkSpeakListen

Why might Chicago today be attractive to new immigrants?

A Tragedy That Brought Change

At the end of the day on March 25, 1911, the women who worked in New York City's Triangle Factory were preparing to go home.... It had been a long day for the workers who cut and sewed fabric to make women's blouses known as shirtwaists.

Just before 5 p.m., shouts of "Fire!" rang out....

Frightened workers rushed to the exits but found many of them locked. There was only one fire escape, and people crowded onto it. The fire escape was worthless, however, as the weight of so many people ripped it off the factory building.... To escape burning to death, many jumped. Within an hour, 146 people perished.

The horrors of that day brought attention to the meager wages and unsafe working conditions many people endured. It led to important changes for workers. Now there are national requirements for minimum wages...and there are strict safety regulations for the workplace.

4. ThinkSpeakListen

What types of regulations might have prevented the tragedy at the Triangle Factory?

Use Irregular Nouns

Sentence	Singular Form	Plural Form
People flocked to this new city, searching for jobs and hoping for a better life.	life	lives
According to the U.S. Census of 1870, nearly 300,000 people called Chicago home.	person	people
The first settler of Chicago was Jean Baptiste Point du Sable…a free black man believed to be born in Haiti or Santo Domingo.	man	men
At the end of the day on March 25, 1911, the women who worked in New York City's Triangle Factory were preparing to go home.	woman	women

5. ThinkSpeakListen

Create new sentences using the plural nouns listed above.

The Great Migration and the Growth of Cities

by Monica Halpern

In 1910, around 7 million of the nation's 8 million African Americans, close to 90 percent, lived in the rural South.

By 1930, between 1.5 and 2 million African Americans had moved to the cities of the North...This movement north was the first wave of what is now referred to as "the Great Migration...."

Why did so many African Americans leave the South? The South was a farming region that depended on one main crop, cotton.

Beginning in 1910, much of the cotton crop was destroyed by the invasion of a tiny insect, the boll weevil. Since most African Americans were farmworkers, the loss of the cotton crop meant the loss of their jobs....

In the North, however, jobs needed to be filled. When World War I started in 1914, it created a huge demand for guns and supplies.

Northern factories needed more workers to supply those war products. Once the United States entered the war, thousands of men enlisted....

The war also created other positions for African Americans. Before the war, new immigrants from European countries filled many of the factory jobs.

Since the United States was now at war with some of those countries, it closed its borders to their citizens. Immigration was halted, presenting job opportunities for African Americans....

6. ThinkSpeakListen

Explain the ways in which World War I affected the Great Migration.

The North also promised greater social and political freedom for African Americans. The Fifteenth Amendment to the Constitution guaranteed the right to vote for African American men in 1870....

However, according to the Smithsonian Institution, most southern states made it very difficult, if not impossible, for African American men to vote....

Most southern states also had segregation laws that required white and black people to be separated in public places....

In the North, African Americans had greater access to public places and activities and felt a greater sense of freedom there.

7. ThinkSpeakListen

Explain how conditions for African Americans were better in the North than in the South during the time of the Great Migration.

Combine Clauses to Condense Ideas

Clauses	Combined into One Sentence
Most African Americans were farmworkers. / The loss of the cotton crop meant the loss of their jobs.	**Since** most African Americans were farmworkers, the loss of the cotton crop meant the loss of their jobs.
Immigration was halted. / This presented job opportunities for African Americans.	Immigration was halted, **presenting** job opportunities for African Americans.
The North also promised greater social freedom for African Americans. / It also promised greater political freedom for African Americans.	The North also promised greater **social and political** freedom for African Americans.
The South was a farming region. / It depended on one main crop. / That crop was cotton.	The South was a farming region **that** depended on one main crop, **cotton**.

8. ThinkSpeakListen

Give some reasons why a writer might want to combine clauses into one sentence.

The Glassblower's Daughter

Every day after school, the bus drops me off at a fascinating place—the Torpedo Factory. Even though it's not a torpedo factory anymore the name stuck. It's an art center now....

I begin, like usual, by making my rounds, popping in to see my friends. Mrs. Alika is painting an ocean storm....

The twin sisters who work there make enormous weavings out of wool, silk, cotton, and even feathers....

At last I reach my mom's studio. It's always warm in there because of the super-hot furnace required to melt the glass. She is twirling a glowing orange orb while blowing into a long metal tube, her breath inflating the glass. A delicate, silvery blue vase starts to form.

9. ThinkSpeakListen

Do you think the workers who built torpedoes at the factory during World War II would be happy to see the factory used for making art? Why or why not?

Research and Writing

Writing Prompt

Research a group of people that migrated from one place to another at some time in America's history (for example: pilgrims, pioneers, African Americans). Imagine that you were a part of this group, and write two or more journal entries describing your experience.

Research Topic

Purpose of Writing

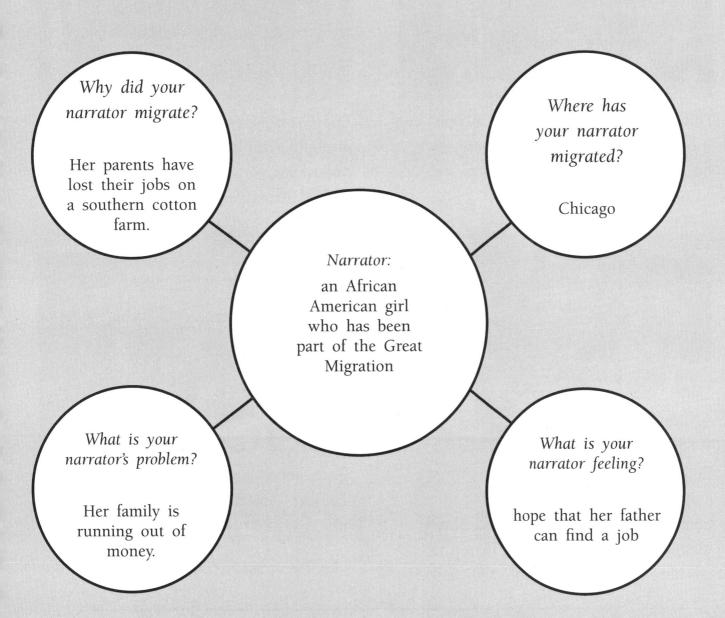

Why did your narrator migrate?

Her parents have lost their jobs on a southern cotton farm.

Where has your narrator migrated?

Chicago

Narrator:

an African American girl who has been part of the Great Migration

What is your narrator's problem?

Her family is running out of money.

What is your narrator feeling?

hope that her father can find a job

Old Cities Revitalize

by Alexandra Hanson-Harding

During World War II, many people had moved to cities to make planes, ships, bombs, and other war products.

The Great Migration from the South brought a million-plus African Americans to the North, changing the face of American cities.

Following World War II, the United States experienced an economic boom. Factories in the United States manufactured automobiles, furniture, clothing, and other products to sell...

Since goods had been so scarce during the war, Americans were now eager to buy....

10. ThinkSpeakListen

Following World War II, how might the economic boom have affected the lives of Americans?

Between 1945 and 1949, Americans purchased 20 million refrigerators and 5.5 million stoves. This trend continued into the 1950s.

As many Americans started to earn more money, they began to leave the cities. Many families moved to newly built suburbs. These communities had better-equipped schools, more open spaces, and homes with yards....

By the late 1960s, many major cities had lost tens of thousands of residents. Factories also began to close or move away.

With fewer people paying taxes, these cities could not provide important services, such as good schools and police protection.

Meanwhile, crime rates rose. As residents felt increasingly unsafe, cities lost more businesses and the population declined further.

Between 1960 and 1980, Detroit lost nearly half a million people. Cleveland and Philadelphia each lost an estimated 300,000.

In the decades since the 1980s, the United States has experienced economic ups and downs.... Still, there are signs that some urban areas are beginning to turn around.

These cities are acting creatively to revitalize their downtowns and attract new businesses and residents.

11. ThinkSpeakListen

Recount the reasons that many people left American cities in the decades following World War II.

Use Introductory Prepositional Phrases to Establish Time

Sentence	Preposition Indicating Time
During World War II, many people had moved to cities to make planes, ships, bombs, and other war products.	During
Following World War II, the United States experienced an economic boom.	Following
By the late 1960s, many major cities had lost tens of thousands of residents.	By
Between 1960 and 1980, Detroit lost nearly half a million people.	Between
In the decades since the 1980s, the United States has experienced economic ups and downs.	In since

12. ThinkSpeakListen

Summarize what you have done today, using some of the prepositions listed above.

Out of Disaster

Look around at your community. Now imagine that nearly all of the places you call home—the familiar houses, schools, parks, buildings, and streets—have been destroyed. That's what happened to Greensburg, Kansas, on May 4, 2007, when a tornado screamed through the town....

After the disaster, officials embarked on a program to inspect the damage and discovered that Greensburg's infrastructure—its roads, water towers, electrical systems—was wiped out. More than 1,400 homes and businesses were permanently destroyed or badly damaged.

The leaders of Greensburg worried that their community might never recover. If it did, it would have to be rebuilt almost entirely as environmentally friendly... making Greensburg among the most environmentally friendly towns in the nation. Using wind, water, and solar power, many buildings use forty percent less energy than they did before the tornado.

13. ThinkSpeakListen

How did the tornado affect Greensburg? How did the city leaders respond to the disaster?

Research and Writing

Writing Prompt

Research a group of people that migrated from one place to another at some time in America's history (for example: pilgrims, pioneers, African Americans). Imagine that you were a part of this group, and write two or more journal entries describing your experience.

Research Topic

Purpose of Writing

Sample Journal Entries

Journal Entry 1

We arrived in Chicago yesterday, and my father went out this morning to look for a job. We hope that he can find one quickly. My family is running out of money.

Establish the situation.

When the boll weevils came and destroyed the cotton crops in the South, my father and mother lost their jobs on the cotton farm in Alabama. We decided that we had to come north, because we'd heard that a lot of factories here were hiring workers. Many of our friends also lost their jobs, and they decided to travel to the North, as well. To save money, we travelled together with them, but we still had to spend nearly all we had on the journey. I hope that my father can find work soon.

Develop events by describing actions, thoughts, and feelings. Show how characters respond to situations.

Journal Entry 2

Luckily, my father was hired last week, on the second day after we arrived here. He will be working at one of the local factories that are producing weapons for American soldiers fighting in Europe. We are greatly relieved that we won't have to worry about money any more.

Resolve the situation and provide a sense of closure.

Essential Question

Why do we measure and describe the world?

My Language Objectives

- Expand noun phrases
- Understand the language of cause and effect
- Switch from present tense to future tense
- Use relative clauses to describe nouns
- Write an opinion essay

My Content Objectives

- Build vocabulary related to the development of chemistry
- Explain why we measure and describe the world

Matter can have different forms.

Matter is made of tiny atoms.

Matter can go through physical and chemical changes.

John Dalton: Father of the Atomic Theory by Kathy Furgang

John Dalton

John Dalton was a renowned nineteenth-century chemist.... Dalton's hard work and persistent focus helped him answer one of the most mysterious questions of all time: "What is the world made of?"...

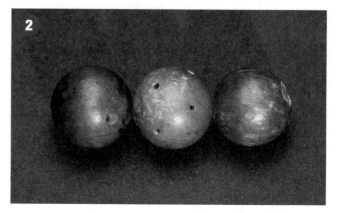

His work established one of the first models of the atom and remains the basis for all modern understanding of matter....

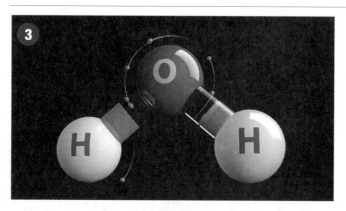

- All matter is composed of tiny particles called atoms.
- All atoms of a given element are identical.
- Atoms cannot be created, destroyed, or subdivided.

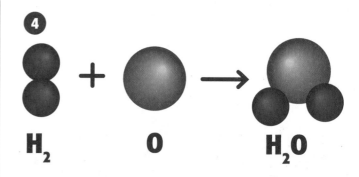

H_2 O H_2O

- Compounds form when atoms of different elements join in fixed ratios.
- A chemical reaction is a rearrangement of atoms, not a change in the atoms themselves.

1. ThinkSpeakListen

How does Dalton's model of the atom help us think about matter?

Expand Noun Phrases

1. Add academic vocabulary

John Dalton was a chemist.

He was renowned.

He lived in the nineteenth century.

John Dalton was <u>a renowned nineteenth-century</u> chemist.

2. Add comparatives and superlatives

Dalton's hard work and persistent focus helped him answer an important question.

The question was one of the most mysterious questions of all time.

Dalton's hard work and persistent focus helped him answer one of <u>the most mysterious questions of all time</u>.

3. Add adjectives and reduced clauses

All matter is composed of particles.

The particles are tiny.

We call these particles atoms.

All matter is composed of tiny particles called atoms.

2. ThinkSpeakListen

Explain why a writer might choose to expand noun phrases.

Matter Is Everywhere!

by Seba Milo

What is matter?... Matter is anything that has mass and volume. Mass is the amount of matter in an object, and volume is the amount of space the object takes up.

Matter is made of tiny particles called atoms.... Matter can exist in three states, or forms: solid, liquid, or gas....

The particles in a solid are packed tightly together, so they can barely move. This gives the solid its fixed shape and volume....

Unlike a solid, the particles in a liquid are not held together tightly, but are farther apart. This means they can slide past one another, which gives liquid a unique property: the ability to flow and take the shape of whatever container it is in....

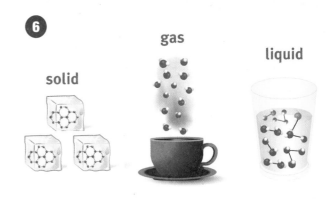

5

6

gas

solid

liquid

The particles in a gas are held together even more loosely than those of a liquid.... For this reason, they can bounce around and expand to fill a very large space, or they can be compressed, or squeezed together, into a much smaller space....

If energy, such as heat, is added to matter, the particles move faster. If energy escapes, the particles slow down. The physical state of matter changes in either case, but the amount of matter remains the same.

7

8

For example, when water, a liquid, is heated to its boiling point, it becomes a gas called steam. When steam, or water vapor, loses energy, it cools and becomes liquid water again.

When the energy in liquid water escapes, it cools. If it reaches its freezing point, it becomes a solid called ice. If heat energy is added to the ice, it melts and becomes liquid water again.

3. ThinkSpeakListen

What happens to water particles when liquid water becomes ice?

Balloon Ride

It is just after sunrise when you enter the field. The dew-dropped grass is damp beneath your feet. The wind is the calmest at this time of day, which is why this is the best time for a hot air balloon flight.... Men, women, and children gather around.

Then, the ground crew begins to spread the brightly colored silken envelope out on the grass.

An inflator fan is placed at the neck, and the balloon starts to fill up with air....

Once the envelope is completely full, you make your way to the basket with the other passengers.

When all the weight is fully balanced, the balloon is detached from the ropes holding it to the floor. The difference in air pressure allows the balloon to rise. The flight is officially underway!... On this clear day you can see for miles. After about an hour, the pilot starts looking for a safe place to land! Good luck!

4. ThinkSpeakListen

Would you like to ride on a hot air balloon? Describe what you think it would be like.

Understand the Language of Cause and Effect

Cause	Effect
If energy, such as heat, is added to matter,	the particles move faster.
If energy escapes,	the particles slow down.
For example, **when** water, a liquid, is heated to its boiling point,	it becomes a gas called steam.
When steam, or water vapor, loses energy,	it cools and becomes liquid water again.
When the energy in liquid water escapes,	it cools.
If it reaches its freezing point,	it becomes a solid called ice.
If heat energy is added to the ice,	it melts and becomes liquid water again.

5. ThinkSpeakListen

Using the language of cause and effect, describe what happens to liquids under very hot conditions and very cold conditions.

Investigate: Changes in Matter

by Laura McDonald

1

Whether a person is making a bed or making a salad, the person is making physical changes to matter.... Chopping a carrot, crushing a can, tearing a piece of paper, and any other changes in shape, size, or texture are physical changes.... Making mixtures and solutions involves other physical changes that can be observed every day....

2

A mixture is a combination of two or more different types of matter.... For instance, to make a salad, a person puts lettuce, tomatoes, and other ingredients together in a bowl....

3

No chemical change is taking place. The lettuce is still lettuce. The person can also separate the salad mixture back into its original parts.

6. ThinkSpeakListen

Think of something you use in school every day, and describe some of the physical changes you can make to it.

When a person drops something into a recycling bin, the person is adding to a mixture.... A recycling center has a complex way of separating the mixture.

First, the mixture is put on a spinning table. The paper and cardboard fall off the table. Everything that is left moves along a conveyor belt.

Next, a magnet pulls out the steel cans. Then, a strong fan blows the plastic into a container.

Finally, the remaining materials are sorted by workers or by an electronic scanner so they, too, can be melted down and recycled.

8 A solution is a special type of mixture in which one substance dissolves into another. The two parts of the mixture are no longer visible....

9 To make a solution, first add a few teaspoons of salt to a cup of water. At first, the salt and the water are still both visible because it's not a solution yet.

10 Next, use a spoon to stir the mixture until the salt disappears. You will observe that the salt is dissolving in the water. When all of the salt dissolves, a saltwater solution will result.

11 Unlike a salad, or a recycling bin, the contents cannot be so easily separated.... One way is evaporation. Pour the saltwater into a shallow pan, and the water in the solution will gradually dry up. The salt will remain in the pan.

7. ThinkSpeakListen

How is a solution different from a mixture?

Switch from Present Tense to Future Tense

Present Tense

A solution is a special type of mixture in which one substance dissolves into another.	
To make a solution, first add a few teaspoons of salt to a cup of water.	

Future Tense

You will observe that the salt is dissolving in the water.	
When all of the salt dissolves, a saltwater solution will result.	
The water in the solution will gradually dry up. The salt will remain in the pan.	

8. ThinkSpeakListen

Why did the author use the future tense at the end of the explanation of how to make a solution?

My Dad the Street Chef

My dad is a street chef. He and other street chefs are now competing for the best food truck in the city. Cooking runs in my family. My grandfather was a street chef, too. He had one of the first propane-fueled portable refrigeration carts in the city.…

Grandpop describes some of the concoctions that street chefs make today and shakes his head in amazement. One game-changing recipe is my dad's mint-and-curry coleslaw. This mixture of chopped cabbage, carrots, mint, and seasoning is mouthwatering. His secret trick is to soak the cabbage in a honey-and-vinegar solution…

Grandpop says this is very different from throwing whatever fresh ingredients they had together and making it work. But Dad is quick to remind him that good cooking is chemistry. No matter where you are in history, the same physical and chemical changes are taking place.

9. ThinkSpeakListen

What is your favorite recipe that includes physical and/or chemical changes?

Research and Writing

Writing Prompt

<u>Research inventions or discoveries made in the field of chemistry over the last 100 years.</u> <u>In your opinion, which invention or discovery has had the greatest impact on people's everyday lives?</u> <u>Write an essay in which you clearly state your opinion and provide supporting reasons and evidence based on your research.</u>

Research Topic

Question

Purpose for Writing

Thesis

Using the properties of silicon microchips to develop the microprocessor has had the greatest impact on our everyday lives, because it makes possible the small computers that we use on a daily basis.

Small Devices at Home

Used for homework:

- calculators
- word processing programs on personal computers

Source: "How Students Today Use Technology"
– *Education Today*

Phones

Used for:

- weather forecasts
- e-mail
- telling time
- games

Source: "Phone Power!"—Hi-Tech.com

Marie M. Daly: Biochemistry Pioneer by Drake Conyers

Marie M. Daly

How do people know which foods are healthful and which are not?... One woman's research profoundly changed people's understanding of how the human body works....

Her curiosity about its complex chemistry helped answer many important questions about health. She studied how the body processes the chemicals in food....

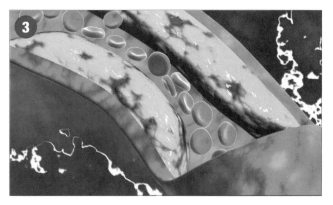

Dr. Marie Maynard Daly...studied the effects of cholesterol on the mechanics of the heart. As a result of this research, she discovered the link between high cholesterol and clogged arteries.

This breakthrough led to a better understanding of how heart attacks are caused.

Daly's research focused on the chemical reactions that take place during food digestion and metabolism....

10. ThinkSpeakListen

Explain why it is important for scientists to ask questions about how the body works.

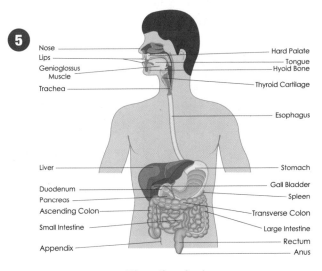

⑤

Nose
Lips
Genioglossus Muscle
Trachea

Hard Palate
Tongue
Hyoid Bone
Thyroid Cartilage

Esophagus

Liver
Duodenum
Pancreas
Ascending Colon
Small Intestine
Appendix

Stomach
Gall Bladder
Spleen
Transverse Colon
Large Intestine
Rectum
Anus

Digestive System

Metabolism describes any reaction by which complex molecules are broken down to produce energy.... The body uses enzymes to break down and digest different food substances. Each enzyme has a specific job.

⑥

Amylase is the enzyme that helps the body process sugars and starches (carbohydrates) like pasta and potatoes.

⑦

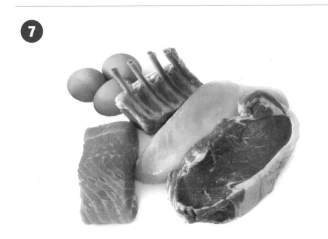

Protease is the enzyme that allows the body to process proteins.

⑧

Lipase is the enzyme that helps break down fats (lipids) found in fatty foods such nuts, meat, and dairy.

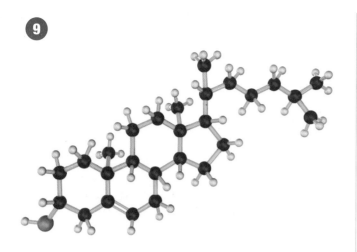

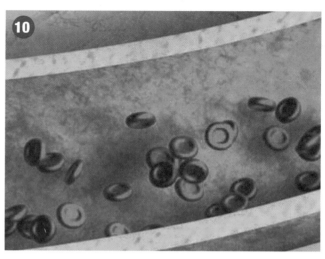

Cholesterol (kuh-LES-tuh-role) is a white, waxy, odorless, and tasteless substance that can be found in all animal tissue…

Cholesterol is essential to life. It helps make up the cell membrane that surrounds each animal cell. It also helps the body process different acids, hormones, and vitamins. It circulates freely in the bloodstream.

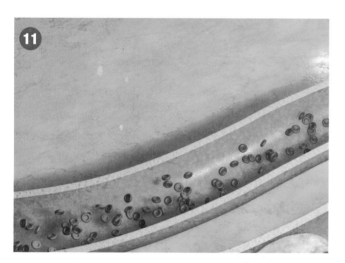

Because many humans eat other animals as part of their daily diet, they consume added cholesterol.… High levels of cholesterol…may cause a buildup…

This buildup in the arteries can lead to blockage that makes it difficult for blood to circulate to the heart and through the body. That is why too much cholesterol causes heart disease and can lead to heart attacks.

11. ThinkSpeakListen

What is one important thing that one can learn from Dr. Daly's research?

Use <u>Relative Clauses</u> to Describe <u>Nouns</u>

Sentence	Noun	Relative Clause
Amylase is the <u>enzyme</u> <u>that helps the body</u> <u>process sugars and starches</u> <u>(carbohydrates) like pasta</u> <u>and potatoes.</u>	<u>enzyme</u>	<u>that helps the body</u> <u>process sugars and starches</u> <u>(carbohydrates) like pasta and</u> <u>potatoes.</u>
Cholesterol is essential to life. It helps make up the <u>cell membrane</u> <u>that</u> <u>surrounds each animal cell.</u>	<u>cell membrane</u>	<u>that surrounds each animal</u> <u>cell.</u>
This buildup in the arteries can lead to <u>blockage</u> <u>that</u> <u>makes it difficult for blood</u> <u>to circulate to the heart</u> <u>and through the body.</u>	<u>blockage</u>	<u>that makes it difficult for</u> <u>blood to circulate to the heart</u> <u>and through the body.</u>

12. ThinkSpeakListen
What types of details can we add to sentences by using relative clauses?

What Makes It Pop?

Popcorn is different from the regular sweet corn we enjoy at meals. It is a type of corn that is grown especially for popping. Each popcorn kernel has a hard shell, or hull, with starch inside. You might not think of a popcorn kernel as moist, but each kernel holds a tiny bit of water. When you heat up a popcorn kernel, the water inside begins to expand. The hull holds in the moisture until its expansion causes a tiny explosion to occur.... The starch inside the kernel has turned to jellylike goo that inflates and spills out. The result is the irregularly shaped snack we call popcorn.

Popcorn has been around for thousands of years.... Native Americans used popcorn for food and as a decoration, too. People still decorate their homes with strings of popcorn on holidays, but the best thing about popcorn is to eat it. Plain, buttered, or flavored, popcorn is a special snack most people just can't resist!

13. ThinkSpeakListen

In every batch of popcorn, there are at least a few kernels that do not pop. Based on what you have learned in this unit, think of different reasons why this happens.

Research and Writing

Research inventions or discoveries made in the field of chemistry over the last 100 years. In your opinion, which invention or discovery has had the greatest impact on people's everyday lives? Write an essay in which you clearly state your opinion and provide supporting reasons and evidence based on your research.

Topic for research/writing

Research focus

Type of writing

Sample Essay

Today we use computers for just about everything. We have personal computers at home and smartphones and tablets for when we go out. We rely on these devices for everything from homework to weather forecasts to communication. But none of this technology would be possible without the microprocessor—and the silicon microchips inside it. The first microprocessor was built in 1971 by Ted Hoff. This development made it possible for computers to be smaller and faster. Using the properties of silicon to develop the microprocessor is therefore the innovation that has had the greatest impact on our everyday lives.

The introduction presents the topic and states an opinion.

Because of microprocessors, computers are now small enough for people to have at home. We are thus able to use them for simple tasks. Homework is one example of a task that we can do easily because we have computers at home. It would be a lot harder to do homework every day without calculators and word processing programs.

Even the computers in our phones are extremely powerful and allow us to do a lot of things. These tiny computers let us check the weather forecast, e-mail our friends, and always know what time it is. We can even play games on them. Without silicon microchips and the microprocessor, these devices would not be possible.

The body paragraphs provide reasons that are supported by details.

The first computers were huge and expensive, and had limited abilities. Because of the invention of the microprocessor in 1971, we now have personal computers and handheld computers that we use every day. And these computers are even more powerful than the one that was used to send astronauts to the moon in 1969! The world would definitely be a different place if the microprocessor had never been invented.

The conclusion restates the main idea and brings the essay to a close.

Common Core State Standards

CA CCSS Reading Standards for Literature

RL.5.1	Quote accurately from a text when explaining what the text says explicitly and when drawing inferences from the text.
RL.5.2	Determine a theme of a story, drama, or poem from details in the text, including how characters in a story or drama respond to challenges or how the speaker in a poem reflects upon a topic; summarize the text.
RL.5.3	Compare and contrast two or more characters, settings, or events in a story or drama, drawing on specific details in the text (e.g., how characters interact).
RL.5.4	Determine the meaning of words and phrases as they are used in a text, including figurative language such as metaphors and similes. **(See grade 5 Language standards 4–6 for additional expectations.) CA**
RL.5.5	Explain how a series of chapters, scenes, or stanzas fits together to provide the overall structure of a particular story, drama, or poem.
RL.5.6	Describe how a narrator's or speaker's point of view influences how events are described.
RL.5.7	Analyze how visual and multimedia elements contribute to the meaning, tone, or beauty of a text (e.g., graphic novel, multimedia presentation of fiction, folktale, myth, poem).
RL.5.9	Compare and contrast stories in the same genre (e.g., mysteries and adventure stories) on their approaches to similar themes and topics.
RL.5.10	By the end of the year, read and comprehend literature, including stories, dramas, and poetry, at the high end of the grades 4–5 text complexity band independently and proficiently.

CA CCSS Reading Standards for Informational Text

RI.5.1	Quote accurately from a text when explaining what the text says explicitly and when drawing inferences from the text.
RI.5.2	Determine two or more main ideas of a text and explain how they are supported by key details; summarize the text.
RI.5.3	Explain the relationships or interactions between two or more individuals, events, ideas, or concepts in a historical, scientific, or technical text based on specific information in the text.
RI.5.4	Determine the meaning of general academic and domain-specific words and phrases in a text relevant to a *grade 5 topic or subject area.* **(See grade 5 Language standards 4–6 for additional expectations.) CA**
RI.5.5	Compare and contrast the overall structure (e.g., chronology, comparison, cause/effect, problem/solution) of events, ideas, concepts, or information in two or more texts.
RI.5.6	Analyze multiple accounts of the same event or topic, noting important similarities and differences in the point of view they represent.
RI.5.7	Draw on information from multiple print or digital sources, demonstrating the ability to locate an answer to a question quickly or to solve a problem efficiently.
RI.5.8	Explain how an author uses reasons and evidence to support particular points in a text, identifying which reasons and evidence support which point(s).
RI.5.9	Integrate information from several texts on the same topic in order to write or speak about the subject knowledgeably.
RI.5.10	By the end of the year, read and comprehend informational texts, including history/social studies, science, and technical texts, at the high end of the grades 4–5 text complexity band independently and proficiently.

CA CCSS Reading Standards for Foundational Skills

RF.5.3	Know and apply grade-level phonics and word analysis skills in decoding words. a. Use combined knowledge of all letter-sound correspondences, syllabication patterns, and morphology (e.g., roots and affixes) to read accurately unfamiliar multisyllabic words in context and out of context.
RF.5.4	Read with sufficient accuracy and fluency to support comprehension. a. Read on-level text with purpose and understanding. b. Read on-level prose and poetry orally with accuracy, appropriate rate, and expression on successive readings. c. Use context to confirm or self-correct word recognition and understanding, rereading as necessary.

CA CCSS Writing Standards

W.5.1	Write opinion pieces on topics or texts, supporting a point of view with reasons and information. a. Introduce a topic or text clearly, state an opinion, and create an organizational structure in which ideas are logically grouped to support the writer's purpose. b. Provide logically ordered reasons that are supported by facts and details. c. Link opinion and reasons using words, phrases, and clauses (e.g., *consequently, specifically*). d. Provide a concluding statement or section related to the opinion presented.
W.5.2	Write informative/explanatory texts to examine a topic and convey ideas and information clearly. a. Introduce a topic clearly, provide a general observation and focus, and group related information logically; include formatting (e.g., headings), illustrations, and multimedia when useful to aiding comprehension. b. Develop the topic with facts, definitions, concrete details, quotations, or other information and examples related to the topic. c. Link ideas within and across categories of information using words, phrases, and clauses (e.g., *in contrast, especially*). d. Use precise language and domain-specific vocabulary to inform about or explain the topic. e. Provide a concluding statement or section related to the information or explanation presented.
W.5.3	Write narratives to develop real or imagined experiences or events using effective technique, descriptive details, and clear event sequences. a. Orient the reader by establishing a situation and introducing a narrator and/or characters; organize an event sequence that unfolds naturally. b. Use narrative techniques, such as dialogue, description, and pacing, to develop experiences and events or show the responses of characters to situations. c. Use a variety of transitional words, phrases, and clauses to manage the sequence of events. d. Use concrete words and phrases and sensory details to convey experiences and events precisely. e. Provide a conclusion that follows from the narrated experiences or events.
W.5.4	Produce clear and coherent writing **(including multiple-paragraph texts)** in which the development and organization are appropriate to task, purpose, and audience. (Grade-specific expectations for writing types are defined in standards 1–3 above.) **CA**
W.5.5	With guidance and support from peers and adults, develop and strengthen writing as needed by planning, revising, editing, rewriting, or trying a new approach. (Editing for conventions should demonstrate command of Language standards 1–3 up to and including grade 5.)
W.5.6	With some guidance and support from adults, use technology, including the Internet, to produce and publish writing as well as to interact and collaborate with others; demonstrate sufficient command of keyboarding skills to type a minimum of two pages in a single sitting.
W.5.7	Conduct short research projects that use several sources to build knowledge through investigation of different aspects of a topic.
W.5.8	Recall relevant information from experiences or gather relevant information from print and digital sources; summarize or paraphrase information in notes and finished work, and provide a list of sources.
W.5.9	Draw evidence from literary or informational texts to support analysis, reflection, and research. a. Apply *grade 5 Reading standards* to literature (e.g., "Compare and contrast two or more characters, settings, or events in a story or a drama, drawing on specific details in the text [e.g., how characters interact]"). b. Apply *grade 5 Reading standards* to informational texts (e.g., "Explain how an author uses reasons and evidence to support particular points in a text, identifying which reasons and evidence support which point[s]").
W.5.10	Write routinely over extended time frames (time for research, reflection, and revision) and shorter time frames (a single sitting or a day or two) for a range of discipline-specific tasks, purposes, and audiences.

CA CCSS Speaking and Listening Standards

SL.5.1	Engage effectively in a range of collaborative discussions (one-on-one, in groups, and teacher-led) with diverse partners on *grade 5 topics and texts*, building on others' ideas and expressing their own clearly. a. Come to discussions prepared, having read or studied required material; explicitly draw on that preparation and other information known about the topic to explore ideas under discussion. b. Follow agreed-upon rules for discussions and carry out assigned roles. c. Pose and respond to specific questions by making comments that contribute to the discussion and elaborate on the remarks of others. d. Review the key ideas expressed and draw conclusions in light of information and knowledge gained from the discussions.
SL.5.2	Summarize a written text read aloud or information presented in diverse media and formats, including visually, quantitatively, and orally.
SL.5.3	Summarize the points a speaker **or media source** makes and explain how each claim is supported by reasons and evidence, **and identify and analyze any logical fallacies. CA**
SL.5.4	Report on a topic or text or present an opinion, sequencing ideas logically and using appropriate facts and relevant, descriptive details to support main ideas or themes; speak clearly at an understandable pace. **a. Plan and deliver an opinion speech that: states an opinion, logically sequences evidence to support the speaker's position, uses transition words to effectively link opinions and evidence (e.g., *consequently* and *therefore*), and provides a concluding statement related to the speaker's position. CA** **b. Memorize and recite a poem or section of a speech or historical document using rate, expression, and gestures appropriate to the selection. CA**
SL.5.5	Include multimedia components (e.g., graphics, sound) and visual displays in presentations when appropriate to enhance the development of main ideas or themes.
SL.5.6	Adapt speech to a variety of contexts and tasks, using formal English when appropriate to task and situation. (See grade 5 Language standards 1 and 3 for specific expectations.)

CA CCSS Language Standards

L.5.1	Demonstrate command of the conventions of standard English grammar and usage when writing or speaking. a. Explain the function of conjunctions, prepositions, and interjections in general and their function in particular sentences. b. Form and use the perfect (e.g., *I had walked; I have walked; I will have walked*) verb tenses. c. Use verb tense to convey various times, sequences, states, and conditions. d. Recognize and correct inappropriate shifts in verb tense. e. Use correlative conjunctions (e.g., *either/or, neither/nor*).
L.5.2	Demonstrate command of the conventions of standard English capitalization, punctuation, and spelling when writing. a. Use punctuation to separate items in a series. b. Use a comma to separate an introductory element from the rest of the sentence. c. Use a comma to set off the words *yes* and *no* (e.g., *Yes, thank you*), to set off a tag question from the rest of the sentence (e.g., *It's true, isn't it?*), and to indicate direct address (e.g., *Is that you, Steve?*). d. Use underlining, quotation marks, or italics to indicate titles of works. e. Spell grade-appropriate words correctly, consulting references as needed.
L.5.3	Use knowledge of language and its conventions when writing, speaking, reading, or listening. a. Expand, combine, and reduce sentences for meaning, reader/listener interest, and style. b. Compare and contrast the varieties of English (e.g., dialects, registers) used in stories, dramas, or poems.
L.5.4	Determine or clarify the meaning of unknown and multiple-meaning words and phrases based on *grade 5 reading and content*, choosing flexibly from a range of strategies. a. Use context (e.g., cause/effect relationships and comparisons in text) as a clue to the meaning of a word or phrase. b. Use common, grade-appropriate Greek and Latin affixes and roots as clues to the meaning of a word (e.g., *photograph, photosynthesis*). c. Consult reference materials (e.g., dictionaries, glossaries, thesauruses), both print and digital, to find the pronunciation and determine or clarify the precise meaning of key words and phrases **and to identify alternate word choices in all content areas. CA**
L.5.5	Demonstrate understanding of figurative language, word relationships, and nuances in word meanings. a. Interpret figurative language, including similes and metaphors, in context. b. Recognize and explain the meaning of common idioms, adages, and proverbs. c. Use the relationship between particular words (e.g., synonyms, antonyms, homographs) to better understand each of the words.
L.5.6	Acquire and use accurately grade-appropriate general academic and domain-specific words and phrases, including those that signal contrast, addition, and other logical relationships (e.g., *however, although, nevertheless, similarly, moreover, in addition*).

California English Language Development Standards

CA ELD Part I: Interacting in Meaningful Ways

ELD.PI.5.1	Exchanging information and ideas with others through oral collaborative discussions on a range of social and academic topics
ELD.PI.5.2	Interacting with others in written English in various communicative forms (print, communicative technology, and multimedia)
ELD.PI.5.3	Offering and supporting opinions and negotiating with others in communicative exchanges
ELD.PI.5.4	Adapting language choices to various contexts (based on task, purpose, audience, and text type)
ELD.PI.5.5	Listening actively to spoken English in a range of social and academic contexts
ELD.PI.5.6	Reading closely literary and informational texts and viewing multimedia to determine how meaning is conveyed explicitly and implicitly through language
ELD.PI.5.7	Evaluating how well writers and speakers use language to support ideas and opinions with details or reasons depending on modality, text type, purpose, audience, topic, and content area
ELD.PI.5.8	Analyzing how writers and speakers use vocabulary and other language resources for specific purposes (to explain, persuade, entertain, etc.) depending on modality, text type, purpose, audience, topic, and content area
ELD.PI.5.9	Expressing information and ideas in formal oral presentations on academic topics
ELD.PI.5.10	Writing literary and informational texts to present, describe, and explain ideas and information, using appropriate technology
ELD.PI.5.11	Supporting own opinions and evaluating others' opinions in speaking and writing
ELD.PI.5.12	Selecting and applying varied and precise vocabulary and language structures to effectively convey ideas

CA ELD Part II: Learning About How English Works

ELD.PII.5.1	Understanding text structure
ELD.PII.5.2	Understanding cohesion
ELD.PII.5.3	Using verbs and verb phrases
ELD.PII.5.4	Using nouns and noun phrases
ELD.PII.5.5	Modifying to add details
ELD.PII.5.6	Connecting ideas
ELD.PII.5.7	Condensing ideas

CA ELD Part III: Using Foundational Literacy Skills

ELD.PIII.5.1	See Appendix A [in *Foundational Literacy Skills for English Learners*] for information on teaching reading foundational skills to English learners of various profiles based on age, native language, native language writing system, schooling experience, and literacy experience and proficiency. Some considerations are: • Native language and literacy (e.g., phoneme awareness or print concept skills in native language) should be assessed for potential transference to English language and literacy. • Similarities between native language and English should be highlighted (e.g., phonemes or letters that are the same in both languages). • Differences between native language and English should be highlighted (e.g., some phonemes in English may not exist in the student's native language; native language syntax may be different from English syntax).

Benchmark ADVANCE

Texts *for* English Language Development

Credits
Editors: Gregory Blume, Marty O'Kane
Contributing Editor: Sunita Apte
Creative Director: Laurie Berger
Designer: Kathryn DelVecchio-Kempa
Production: Kosta Triantafillis
Director of Photography: Doug Schneider
Photo Assistant: Jackie Friedman

Photo credits: Cover E: © Sean Sprague / Alamy; Page 2, 8c: World History Archive/Newscom; Page 3a, 4c, 9a, 7b, 18b, 20c: ASSOCIATED PRESS; Page 3b, 9e, 9f, 10C, 14b, 20b: Granger, NYC; Page 6a, 10b: © CORBIS; Page 6b, 10d, 13c, 16b: © Everett Collection Historical / Alamy; Page 6d: Danny Moloshok; 7d: © Flip Schulke/CORBIS; Page 10a, 11a, 13a: © North Wind Picture Archives / Alamy; Page 12b: Picture History/Newscom; Page 14a: © Mary Evans Picture Library / Alamy; Page 16d: Joe Scherschel / contributor; Page 20a: AP Photo/ Evan Vucci; Page 40b: Granger, NYC; Page 43a: © Charles E. Rotkin/CORBIS; Page 46c, 47a, 50a: © North Wind Picture Archives; Page 51d: Granger, NYC; Page 60a: © M Stock / Alam; Page 42: © North Wind Picture Archives; Page 65c: © CORBIS; Page 66b, 67a, 67b, 67c, 67d, 68b, 69a, 74b: Granger, NYC; Page 66c: ullstein bild / Granger, NYC; Page 68a: Rue des Archives / Granger, NYC; Page 86c: Eli Whitney's (1765-1825) Cotton Gin, 1793 (engraving), American School, (18th century) / Private Collection / Peter Newark American Pictures / Bridgeman Images; Page 87a: Everett Collection/Newscom; Page 87d: Spinning cotton with self-acting mules of type devised by Richard Roberts (1825). These could be powered by water wheel or steam engine and power transferred to machines through belt-and-shafting. Under mule minded by woman on left, child is employed to crawl under threads and sweep up. Print c1835. / Universal History Archive/UIG / Bridgeman Images; Page 88a, 93, 100a, 100b, 101b: Granger, NYC; Page 88b: Weaving shed fitted with Jacquard power looms. Swags of punched cards carrying pattern being woven are at right and above each loom. Illustration Paris c1880 / Universal History Archive/ UIG / Bridgeman Images; Page 90b: Erskine Beveridge & Company's Factory, United Kingdom / Universal History Archive/UIG / Bridgeman Images; Page 91: General View of Stockport, Lancashire showing cotton mills, published by J.C. Varrall (fl.1815-27) 1830s (litho), Pickering, George (1794-1857) (after) / Private Collection / Ken Welsh / Bridgeman Images; Page 92: © Heritage Image Partnership Ltd / Alamy; Page 94b: Cristina Muraca/ss.com; Page 96a: Weaving on Power Looms, Cotton factory floor, engraved by James Tingle (fl.1830-60) c.1830 (litho), Allom, Thomas (1804-72) (after) / Private Collection / Ken Welsh / Bridgeman Images; Page 97b,101a: © Mark Harvey / Alamy; Page 98d akg-images/Newscom; Page 98e: ullstein bild / Granger, NYC ; Page 103b MARK THIESSEN/National Geographic Creative; Page 122: © Niday Picture Library / Alamy Stock Photo; Page 123A: Granger, NYC — All rights reserved; Page 124B: SHAH MARAI / Getty Staff; Page 124A: Jeff Mauritzen; Page 127D: MPI / Stringer; Page 129: Louis S. Glanzman / Contributor; Page 131A: Joseph Sohm / Shutterstock. com; Page 131C: © CORBIS; Page 132B, 133: DEA PICTURE LIBRARY / Contributor; Page 134A: Jay P. Morgan; Page 140A: © Ken Davies/Demotix/Corbis; Page 143a: Granger, NYC; Page 147c: © Ros Drinkwater / Alamy; Page 158c: © Andy Fletcher / Alamy; Page 164a, 166c, 170b, 170d, 171c, 172b, 172c, 172d, 176b: Granger, NYC; Page 164b: © National Geographic Image Collection / Alamy; Page 164c: © Bettmann/Corbis; Page 164d: © North Wind Picture Archives / Alamy; Page 166a: © liszt collection / Alamy; Page 168a: © ZUMA Press, Inc / Alamy; Page 168b: © Underwood & Underwood/Corbis; Page 170a: © Everett Collection Inc / Alamy; Page 170c: © Nigel Cattlin / Alamy; Page 171d: © Bettmann/CORBIS; Page 172a: © North Wind Picture Archives / Alamy; Page 176a: © DIZ Muenchen GmbH, Sueddeutsche Zeitung Photo / Alamy; Page 16c: © CAMERIQUE/ClassicStock/Corbis; Page 177a: © H. ARMSTRONG ROBERTS/Corbis; Page 177c: © ClassicStock / Alamy; Page 177d: Glasshouse Images / Glasshouse Images; Page 180b: © Mike Theiss/Ultimate Chase/Corbis; Page 183a, 190d: © ZUMA Press, Inc / Alamy; Page 184c,186b 187a, 187b, 187d: Granger, NYC; Page 186a: ullstein bild / Granger, NYC; Page 188c: © Zoonar GmbH / Alamy; Page 194a: REUTERS/ Chip East; Page 194b: © Marco Destefanis / Alamy; Page 194c: © imageBROKER / Alamy; Page 196a: © Oscar White/CORBIS; Page 196b, 197, 198a: ©TM Rube Goldberg Inc.; Page 196c: © JetPilot / Stockimo / Alamy; Page 200a, 200b: Tony Kyriacou/REX

Art credits: Page 34: Sophie Escabasse; Page 48: Stefano Tambellini; Page 54: Caroline Romanet; Page 104-105: Fermin Solis; Page 106-107: Sophie Escabasse; Page 108: Laura Horton; Page 131-132: Ovi Hondru; Page 144: Juanbjuan Oliver; P148: Bill Greenhead; Page 150-152: Stefano Tambellini; Page 154: Juanbjuan Oliver

Permissions: "I, Too" from The Collected Poems of Langston Hughes by Langston Hughes, edited by Arnold Rampersad with David Roessel, Associate Editor, copyright © 1994 by the Estate of Langston Hughes. Used by permission of Alfred A. Knopf, an imprint of the Knopf Doubleday Publishing Group, a division of Random House LLC. All rights reserved. Excerpt from My Name is America: The Journal of Wong Ming-Chung by Laurence Yep. Copyright © 2000 by Laurence Yep. Reprinted by permission of Scholastic Inc. Excerpt from Zora And Me. Copyright © 2011 by Victoria Bond and T.R. Simon Reproduced by permission of the publisher Candlewick Press, Inc., Somerville, MA. Excerpt from Esperanza Rising by Pam Munoz Ryan. Copyright © 2000 by Pam Munoz Ryan. Reprinted by permission of Scholastic Inc. Excerpt from Julie of the Wolves, text copyright © 1972 by Jean Craighead George. Used by permission of HarperCollins Publishers. "The First Airplane" copyright © 2003 by The American Chemical Society. "Did Farmers of the Past Know More Than We Do?" from The New York Times, November 3, 2012, copyright © 2012 The New York Times Company. All rights reserved.

ISBN: 978-1-5021-6647-0 (hardcover)
ISBN: BE2778 (paperback)